Sinai Victory

Other Books by S. L. A. Marshall

On Tactics and Leading:

MEN AGAINST FIRE

THE ARMED FORCES OFFICER

THE SOLDIER'S LOAD

On Battle:

THE RIVER AND THE GAUNTLET

BASTOGNE: THE FIRST EIGHT DAYS

ISLAND VICTORY

PORK CHOP HILL

MAKIN

On War:

ARMIES ON WHEELS

BLITZKRIEG

On Operations:

CRITIQUE OF INFANTRY OPERATIONS IN KOREA

HILL 440

GUIDE TO THE OCCUPATION OF ENEMY TERRITORY

GUIDE TO THE USE OF INFORMATION MATERIALS

and various other Department of the Army
manuals and operational narratives

SINAI VICTORY

Command Decisions in History's Shortest War,
Israel's Hundred-Hour Conquest of Egypt
East of Suez, Autumn, 1956

by

S. L. A. MARSHALL

Military Critic, *The Detroit News*
Brigadier General, USAR

Maps and Drawings by

H. GARVER MILLER, ORO

WILLIAM MORROW AND COMPANY
New York 1958

To the three Little Women who
call themselves Old Gog, Widow Cakes and Mr. Poogity

Contents

8   CONTENTS

List of Maps

Preface

THERE are subjects about which it is impossible to be accurate. One of them is the spelling of place names in the Middle East. However harshly the syllables of Schenectady and Keokuk may fall upon the nonresident's ear, he is at least blessed in that he need not stay in doubt about how to spell them in the one right way. The same is not true of political geography east of Suez. "Baghdad" is sometimes "Bagdad." "Iraq" is sometimes spelled with a *k* and there are authorities who insist that Aqaba without a *u* looks positively indecent.

One trouble is that the regional maps vary strangely in the spellings used to designate a particular place. The variations are largely according to the period in which the work was done and according to the survey or publishing auspices. When maps are thus foolishly inconsistent, it is vain for people who read them to try to appear wise.

Toward relieving the quandary, the most practical, if more craven, course is simply to acknowledge the problem, systematize nothing and thereby arrive at a solution through compromise which in the end will be acceptable to no one but the author. That is what has been done. Many maps and regional guides have been opened or unfolded and looked at, if not exactly studied until the midnight oil burned low. It was soon learned that they agreed only in the uniformity of their disagreement; even the operations maps used by the Israel Army did not spell all place names alike.

Due to this lack of any standard with a universal sanction, the rule followed in this writing, and by its cartographer, H. Garver Miller, was to take arbitrarily from one source or another that spelling which rides closest to the way the name is pronounced by the majority of informed people in the region.

That could be a loss to the exercising of the alphabet, though the chance of an offsetting gain to the understanding of the possible reader need not be overlooked. It is easier to swallow "Abu Agueila" than to gargle "Abu Aweigila," and "Queisima" is no more sweet when spelled "Quesima" or "Quisaima." As for "E Tour" versus "El Tour," "Elat" when contrasted with "Eilat," or "Rahfa" alongside of "Rafa" or "Rafah," one may only take refuge in the couplet written many years ago:

> If I should knock the "h" from Ghent,
> Some fool will wonder where it went.

But there are other more profound points which are equally undisturbing. The "Dyka Pass" is sometimes written "Daika Pass" and the "Mitla" appears as "Mitle" on several of the older maps. That cuts against the grain, since any way that opens to man in such inhospitable country should be entitled to know its own name. What is called "Parker's Memorial" in this book, and is herein pictured, is described in a reliable source as a monument to the memory of Col. A. C. Palmer, DSO, a valiant British officer who was twice governor of Sinai. But the troops who went there insisted on calling it "Parker's Memorial" however it was dedicated, and they certainly knew where they were going. The late Colonel Palmer should not mind that, in rehallowing the spot, they were a mite careless about its name.

These points aside, the book must stand on its own. Little of it was drawn from official records. Israel's Army is better at fighting than at writing reports thereof for the national archives. No one who has ever tried to square a war diary or after-action report with what he has seen on the fire field will deem this an irreparable loss to man's store of dependable combat knowledge. Truth, with greater accuracy, is spoken by soldiers still under the spell of their battlefield experience.

Many of Israel's most introspective soldiers helped this writing immeasurably by talking things out. One of them was Brig. Gen. Meier Amit. But to two of them especially, Col. Katriel Salmon and Lieut. Col. "Benz" Tehan, my debt is profound, not merely because of their patience and wisdom, but because out of their generous natures they gave me cherished friendship. It was from knowing Katriel first that I wished to know his country.

Other acknowledgments which should be made now will be remembered too late. In the writing of any book there is always this cause for regret. Many hearts and minds make the work possible, but the credit may never be evenly shared.

Still, there must be one last honorable mention. Compared to all else that I owe my wife and partner, Cate Marshall, her contribution to this book is a small thing, indeed. She merely rescued and organized the field notes, prodded me until I was compelled to shape them into narrative, thereafter typed them into manuscript and, last, sat as the first reader and critic of what had been written. Her joy in doing it is the happiest reward that may come of this labor.

S. L. A. MARSHALL

Birmingham, Michigan
May 1958

Sinai Victory

1...The 100-Hour War

THOUGH it is long since I last saw the Sinai Peninsula, where in November and December, 1956, I spent six weeks studying the 100-Hour War fought in the autumn of that year, I am still often asked by Americans, "How could it happen?" "How did Israel's Army do it?"

When in the second year that followed the campaign I spoke at the NATO Defense College on a subject in no way related to the Middle East situation, the first question asked by a member of the audience was, "What is the secret of Israeli mobility?"

By the time of my return from Sinai, my field notes on the battlefield operations were almost complete. More impressive than all else in the combat record was the consistency in all forces, the extraordinary boldness in planning at all levels, the sustained momentum of offensive power and an extreme vigor in ranks when under fire which kept the attack moving according to plan.

Still, one year after that I went back to Israel, not simply because I enjoy its people and their country vastly, but so that I might become more fully informed about the doctrine of Israel's General Staff and the Army way of training.

In Sinai, the action of Israel's soldiers was distinguished by a uniform decisiveness—the ability to give an intrepid order almost instantly or to move on impulse against danger with no hesitation. If the character of the force in combat reflected directly and in accurate proportion what the training system sought to make of its human material, there might be lessons out of Sinai of interest to soldiers everywhere.

This book and its conclusions are the product of the two visits during which I was generously helped by my military hosts, who seem, as a breed, incapable of double talk or dissembling. They are tidy-minded men who mistrust generalities and are more interested in the clear expression of ideas than in the intricacies of argument.

My conclusion while in Sinai—and it stays unchanged—is that Israel's Army did it by extending the limits of military daring. Hitting forces traveled farther over more formidable country in less time than any other combat body in history. Decision was won in three days. By the fourth day some of the brigades (the Israeli term for regiment) were mopping up two hundred miles beyond their assembly points.

This alone is a feat at which to marvel. A fortified area about half the size of Nevada and far more repellent than the harshest wastes in that state was conquered by a small field army fighting as it drove forward almost at the rate of an unopposed motor caravan. Even the few paved roads in Sinai lack level gradients and follow a tortuous course according to the rise and fall of the land.

Almost nowhere is Sinai flat, hard-surfaced desert ·such as is to be found in the American Southwest. Geological features make it virtually a barrier to motorized travel. Saw-toothed ranges cover the southern half of the peninsula and extend their northern fingers almost to the Mediterranean coast. Where the north desert is not irrupted by mountainous dunes, the sand on the flat is everywhere loose. No grass grows in Sinai. The few shrubs rarely stand more than hand high. Save for an occasional jackal or raven there is no wildlife to be seen. Away from the coastal towns only about sixteen thousand people, mostly Bedouins, find it possible to live on the country. Of this land little comes to man but trouble.

The mediocrity of the opposition had something to do with the phenomenal pace of the invading army. But it is only through the close-range view that the opposite and more significant truth stands clear: *the soldiers of Israel invariably looked their best in those hours when they were beset by the greatest combat difficulty and the enemy pressure became such that total disorganization should have ensued.*

Motorization and tracks made possible the record marks in mobility. Without tanks, without half-tracks, Israel's Army could not have started. But there is no bright new magic in that. The United States Army, which has had such vehicles for a generation, has not assured itself the same sustained mobility.

What made the difference? Certainly not professional zeal and efficiency, for Israel's Army is not professional in the way Western nations use that term. The campaign was not aided by any new secret making possible a more adequate supply in the fighting zone. Israel's ranks are not particular wizards at motor maintenance and battlefield repair.

To the contrary. Israel's Staff professes an ignorance of logistics, which in more sophisticated circles has become a kimonolike word, covering everything and touching nothing. Staff members claim—so earnestly as to invite skepticism— that the governing principle is to "send the combat force against the decisive object and then order the supply people to keep up."

Within their training system there is relatively little schooling in the problems of field maintenance, and in the field no such elaborate echeloning of technical skills and parts stores as we know. During fighting operations the fighters do most of the repair. They explain, "Many of us are farmers. We learn the knack on trucks and tractors."

Briefly then, Israel's Army is a fighting body in spirit and not a balanced aggregation of highly trained specialists. In a frontier sort of way, it looks the part. Its men are clean but not neat. From top to bottom, the establishment has no frills of any kind. The office of the Chief of Staff is a bare-walled cubicle. No elevator operates in its many-storied headquarters building. All ranks wear only the austere, rough woolen field uniform.

Smartness in dress is impossible. Smartness in bearing is given only lip service. By Western standards, this Army, while radiating human warmth and the high courtesy native to the country, is wholly lacking in the outward forms of discipline. An enlisted man may appear unshaven, with his hair looking as if he is on strike against the barber. The man on sentry go may be seen munching an orange as he walks his post. An officer may wear striped civilian socks with his suit.

All that counts is the end object which discipline elsewhere is supposed to serve—undeviating performance of the task. Israel gets that from its soldiers without polish or spit, except as the latter is applied to the hands. During the Sinai campaign troops had a saying: "Fear of the higher command is worse than fear of the enemy." It came strangely from the lips of singularly relaxed soldiers. But the exaggerated quip underscores the standard of I-command-you-obey which the Army's doctrine exalts as the fundamental of fighting efficiency.

Its deviations from traditional military practice seem perfectly suited to the temper of a force which is more civilian than soldier. Israel's so-called "Regular Army" is scarcely more than a cadre of higher NCO's, warrant officers and those relatively few commissioned people who love the military life, have demonstrated superior skills and are therefore asked to renew their contracts periodically. There is no enlisted volunteering. The body of the "Regular Army" is that draft of inductees which happens to be getting its two and one-half years' steady training in the going period.

Recruit training is threefold tougher than in the United States Army. But the only stiffness is in the soldier's aching back after a full day. Men salute—occasionally. Orders and directions are stated in the simplest words possible, with a minimum use of technical phrases. The recruit hardly puts on his soldier suit before he learns to refer to his highest commanders by their first names. Within the officer corps the habit of using nicknames is so ingrained that proper names are too often forgotten. One Assistant Chief of Staff explained the high degree of co-ordination in Israel's battle forces in these words, mystifying in their simplicity: "We give and take more easily because we're all friends."

This Army, composed for the great part of men who had to spring from the plow or rush from the office, was given only three days to form and move on Sinai. In that time, its reservists had to assemble, equip, deploy and get such limbering-up training en route as the hours permitted. Brigade and battalion commanders were read into the plan only after mobilization and movement were well under way. With rare exceptions, their own parts, including sectors and in some cases main objectives, were not preassigned. They still had to shape their attack plans, contrive such basic reconnoitering as was possible and issue their orders.

On still another count, as to infantry-armor action, the campaign was unique. Commanders were told to keep battle losses minimal and not encumber their columns with prisoners if it was more opportune to let them get away. All efforts were to be directed toward squeezing out and destroying opposing fortifications. This stricture, imposed because it suited both the political nature of the fighting problem and the moral standard of Israel's troops, made an utmost requirement of movement, while lessening the normal accent on fire.

It would work if communications held up most of the time and if the Egyptians, with their advantages of owning the high ground, where they were relatively safe under deep earth cover, fronting flat fields of fire, were not overly resolute. Both calculations proved accurate. Communications broke down a few times, and usually, as is to be expected, at the highest pitch of the local fire fight. The Egyptians broke down more frequently, giving way time and again in these same minutes of heaviest pressure.

Strength overcame disorganization because Israel's Army fights that way. When the attack becomes disjointed, when radios are muted by fire and lower commands are out of touch with the steadying hand higher up, Israel's soldiers nearest the enemy invariably follow their standard procedure. They close upon the defender's works.

That is the main lesson from the battle story. The phenomenal mobility of Israel's Army isn't generated out of machine power but out of the unanimous acceptance and application of a fighting doctrine which of its essence becomes unifying in the hour of greatest danger. Gideon's band may have held to the same simple rules. There is not one new idea in the doctrine. The startling tactical pace of the Army comes of applying sedulously those methods and precepts which all armies tell their infantry and armor will best maintain unity in battle. The difference is that Israel's soldiers hear and believe.

It's a short list.

. . . Leading means moving to the point of main danger if decisive pressure is to be maintained. There is no excuse for holding back.

. . . When orders can't get through, assume what the orders would be.

. . . When in doubt, hit out. The short route to safety is the road to the enemy hill.

. . . Don't attack head-on; there is usually a better way.

. . . If you must go in head-on, don't present a broad target.

. . . When troops are truly exhausted, hold back and rest them.

. . . Waste no energy in useless movement. Maintain the pace of the attack so long as physical resources seem sufficient.

. . . If the force designated to attack is not suitably armed to overrun the position, pull off and call for what is needed. Avoid useless wastage.

. . . Don't delay the battle because of supply shortages which lie beyond its probable crisis.

. . . Keep your sense of humor if you would save your wits.

. . . When trapped by sudden fire, movement means salvation more surely than a foxhole.

. . . Always try for surprise in one form or another.

. . . When local surprise is possible, don't expose movement with premature fires.

. . . In the attack, risk, risk, risk.

Israel put nine brigades into Sinai. All but one were used in combat; the extra brigade arrived too late. There were two main battles, one of which decided the campaign as a whole. Eight brigades engaged in sharp and casualty-laden actions and wore through approximately a score of moderate-to-heavy skirmishes, without violating any of the combat commandments. Of the eight brigades, only three were "Regular Army."

By Israel Army's tables of organization, a brigade is not heavyweight. Think of a United States regiment at peacetime strength level; the head count is about the same. The brigade of armor musters one battalion of medium tanks (modernized Shermans), one of light tanks (French AMX's), one of lorried infantry, and organic complements of signals, pioneers, medical and headquarters units. The commander may use his battalions separately or split them three ways to form composite teams, as he likes it, or as the target would seem to require. The infantry brigade is not radically different from the U.S. infantry regiment in manpower, though it possesses fewer organic heavy weapons.

One artillery battalion (25-pounders) is usually in direct support of one brigade during battle. If two brigades operate jointly in the attack, another artillery battalion may be on call from higher headquarters. For the average company assault against a fortified position, the covering fire will be provided by one battery. Israel's Army is parsimonious with artillery shell. It is short of what we consider essentials—rounds such as smoke and flares. These played little or no part in the Sinai campaign and the effects of Israeli high explosive, fired by conventional batteries against the Egyptian heavy works, were marginal. The main positions were not knocked down, nor their guns destroyed, either by barrage or by air strafing. With rare exceptions, they went out of action when foot soldiers and armor moving together overran the surrounding works.

The broad design for the campaign as drawn by the High Command was all-inclusive. That is to say that by its end, within less than one week after the first shot was fired, the nine brigades were to stand unchallenged over the whole of Sinai, with every enemy position taken and all resistance ended. All of this was "according to plan." The remnants of Egypt's Army withdrew to the Canal only after its brigades had been broken in trying to hold their defenses. The battlefield story is the final refutation to President Nasser's claim that Israel's swift advance was a hollow victory because he had ordered his Army out of Sinai. Thereby he discredits his troops, most of whom tried to hold their ground, and some of whom fought bravely, although their commanders showed no initiative whatever.

Egypt's Army east of the Canal was formed of the Eighth Palestine Division (not full-strength) in the Gaza-Rahfa area and the Third Division deployed between El Arish and Abu Agueila. Westward of Abu Agueila, between Bir Hamm and Bir Gifgafa, was one brigade of armor. An infantry brigade held high ground blocking the desert road to the port of Suez. Spread over other commanding features of the more central terrain was the Light Mobile Frontier Force, mounted on armored jeeps and troop carriers. Egyptian conscripts are drawn mainly from the fellaheen or farm laborers. The fellah is illiterate, not interested in fighting, lacking any real bond with his officers, and so undernourished that he is not really combat material.

But at least these forces had numbers, solid earth and concrete protection, favorable defensive ground invariably fronting on flat fields of fire, and sufficient modern arms to annihilate infantry and perforate medium armor. At all main positions—as postbattle inspection revealed—the Egyptians were overgunned and overmunitioned. The holding forces were to be uprooted, and not merely routed but so cleared away that, between Sabbaths, the Sinai would be swept clean of them. It was quite an order. The armored ridges were engineered for all-around defense and enclosed by broad belts of barbed wire and mine fields.

The swift, total sweep was envisaged in the plan. The first move was to be the dropping of a paratroop battalion at the Mitla Pass east of Suez, followed by reinforcement of the drop by the rest of the paratroop brigade advancing across country. It would attack through Kuntilla, which is just across the border from the southern Negev, and after overrunning the fortified posts of Themed and Nakhl, would proceed to the linkup.

For twenty-four hours following the drop, the Sinai-bound

field army would not give battle. Coiling tighter during this pause, it would not spring. The High Command hoped by this stratagem to keep Egypt and the world guessing about its intentions, thereby unsteadying the enemy garrisons all along the front.

But there was one exception. To provide a covering shoulder for the opening maneuver by the paratroopers, another brigade would cross the frontier coincidentally in the central sector and capture the key road juncture at Queisima. From there, infantry support, or armor should it be needed, could be sent south to reinforce the Mitla strike, if it drew an Egyptian counter from Bir Gifgafa to the north or from Suez to the west.

With two exceptions, the other brigades in the force held on leash already had firm assignments. When and where they would hit was not contingent on whether the Mitla Pass probe fared well or badly. In the hour of full-scale operations, a vital triangle of enemy defenses in northeast Sinai would be the main target. Its points were the town of Rahfa and the city of El Arish on the north coast and the deserted village of Abu Agueila on the Ismailia road. The ridges which protect Abu Agueila have been used as military strong points since Nabatean times. There, as at El Arish and Rahfa, the Egyptian fortifications which covered the main road in depth were anchored on impassable dunes which made defiles of the thoroughfares. Main Egyptian deployable strength lay within the triangle, as did the military repair shops and supply stores. Behind it were the Egyptian air bases in Sinai.

The battle went as planned, or hoped, or maybe better. The southern paratroop brigade completed its fighting march unaided. Slightly delayed, an infantry brigade captured Queisima. Out of Queisima, an armored brigade moved against Abu Agueila and for three days squeezed it with fire until the position became lifeless. The two brigades—one infantry, one

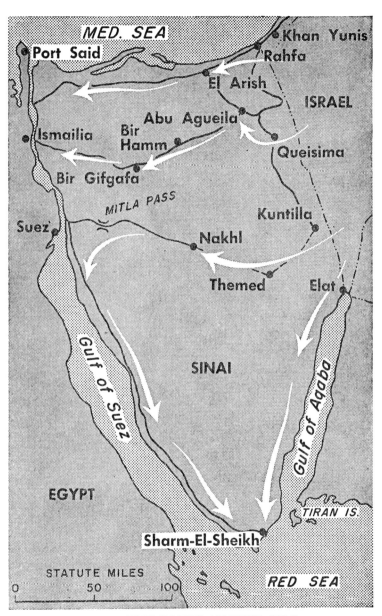

MOVEMENT IN THE 100-HOUR WAR

armor—which captured the fortified sand hills south of Rahfa, thereafter forked. The armor took El Arish and at last halted just east of the Canal. The infantry turned back to police the Gaza Strip, after still another brigade had subdued it.

On these three axes, not one of the columns lost momentum or stayed the attack for more than three hours at any time, save to sleep the men briefly, or to await supply when fuel and ammunition became spent. And this happened not once but several times. Commanders ordered troops to advance even when the risk of becoming stranded was self-apparent.

How the fighting was maintained in each sector, and the pivotal decisions at all levels which gave it direction and vigor, will be better understood as this story unfolds. What a few men thought and dared to order is perhaps more instructive than what many men did. The campaign was won in a whirl by such slender forces that it is almost a miracle they were not beaten by space alone. They did it on nerve more than with fire and deception. It does not cheapen their performance that the resistance was spotty: full courage is not a relative thing. The record is not without blemish. Here and there a leader hesitated, either trying to command from too far back or bending his ear more to the beat of danger than to the call of tactical opportunity. When detected, he was relieved. No excuses tolerated. No explanations asked.

Israel's High Command says: "Success comes when leaders lead instead of pushing." The Army guides by that rule on the battlefield. Squad, platoon and company commanders go first into the fire. Should the attack temporarily stall because of strong resistance, or become unhinged from severed communications, battalion and brigade commanders go posthaste to the center of action and restore movement. If there are two points of disarrangement, the second in command also goes forward.

In the Sinai campaign, these personal-risk missions seldom recatalyzed the attack. The reason is that the people lower down had already acted strongly to restore movement. Would they take hold as vigorously unless they knew that the boss man would soon be there? is a good question.

Measured in bodies only, the cost of this code comes high. Of Israel's soldiers killed in the Sinai war (less than two hundred) half were leaders. Yet the Army believes that this ratio of expendability among its best-qualified fighters is more to be honored than deplored. The Staff says: "That kind of leading, exemplified at all levels, inspires more men to become leaders."

What is reported in this book tends to sustain that view. Mobile in the extreme, the campaign was made so in part by the linking of adroit movement with extraordinary economy of fire. It was in no sense a cut-and-dried, factory-contrived victory. A bit too patronizingly, experts writing about the military power balance in the Middle East tend to stress the great superiority of Israel to its neighbors in the count of fighting machines. This is an oversimplification which ignores the controlling fact that whether one may apply more power or less at the decisive point is according to the radius of operations. There are always roads to be blocked, patrols to be made and mopping-up tasks to be completed lest flanks become exposed and the rear overrun.

Perhaps more significant than the straight narration of how these manual tasks were managed is the rather clear indication, out of this campaign, that in the fighting man unusual physical endurance seems ever the by-product of sustained spiritual boldness. One other highlight deserves equal attention: though physical fitness in ranks and an intrepidity of decision in command, which at times bordered on recklessness, set the pace of the battle, Israel's Army seemed to be acutely sensitive to the limits of its human material. There are many shining examples in the campaign of commanders pausing deliberately in the crisis of action to rest their troops.

Over the world the operation which swept Sinai clean has been praised by soldiers as a "masterpiece of mobility." Statistics support the description. But statistics never win a battle. The proof of whether the masterpiece was made by the mobile mind and the willing heart rather than by the machine is to be found only in the small picture of the fire fighting. The men of this small army did the best possible with what they had. They responded as if what is all-important is to live life fully while one may. To regard their effort in any other light is to miss what counted most in the Sinai adventure.

After completing my field work, I talked to Maj. Gen. Moshe Dayan. We exchanged impressions of the battle. He wanted to know what I had learned about his Army. I told him he should be most satisfied with the fact that at all levels leadership was intent on energizing the fight, but that it first sought to learn what was happening to men. All hands were ready to gamble. But they did not risk blindly. They gave orders only after doing their best to learn the odds. That was why so many leaders died. They went forward to learn rather than to try to play the hero.

Dayan said, "What gratifies me most is that we lost but one prisoner. He was the pilot wounded and brought down behind enemy lines with no chance to escape. That kind of score is no accident. It means that all men were trying, that all believe in the military worth of this army."

Possibly we were using different words to express the same general idea—that the contagion of courage is the source of all battlefield unity, that the power of decision has no other essence than the acceptance of superb risk and that action itself increases mental resilience to a degree unsuspected until it is experienced. Military history reveals this truth on every page, and its most recent chapter, written in the Sinai sands, is but another object lesson in the binding and uplifting effect on military forces which comes of the bold gamble. The immediate corollary to this is the weakening influence of the merely calculated, rationally planned way of doing things.

Where there is no marching bravely into the dark, no noble but ungrounded venture of faith, the word "decision" is hardly justified, either in combat or in the smaller affairs of life. One doesn't decide where to walk if the path is well indicated, or how to get there if the course can be determined through staff argument or the feeding of numbers into a machine.

True decision, by its nature, in combat and elsewhere, consists in determining a line of action when choices are equally difficult. All war is a gamble. Its chief prizes fall only to the player who, weighing the odds carefully as he moves from situation to situation, will not hesitate to plunge when he feels by instinct that his hour has arrived.

Of necessity military training systems instill in leaders respect for the high virtues of careful planning and closely reasoned estimates as a basis for action. This is the main stream of all education preparatory to battle. If any other course were taken, military forces could not even conduct an approach march in an orderly manner, and their hopes would be at the mercy of the most impetuous but thoughtless spirits among them.

But there always comes a time in battle when the most careful planner must also be foremost in willingness to take a superb risk if there is to be inspired leading toward the desired object at minimum cost. The ablest young battalion and company commanders that are to be met in combat are men of this type. They are sedulous in planning and preparation. They make their dispositions painstakingly. They insist on personal reconnaissance to a point where it nettles their subordinates. Thus they have at all times the feel of their own situation, which is one half the battle. But at the opportune moment they are ready to "shoot the works."

This is the essence of real generalship at all levels. It is a quality of the spirit that any man may bring forward in himself, provided that he has become truly the master of his work. But if he is careless of detail, his spirit will be possessed of a false bravado, rather than a well-placed self-confidence, and he cannot even make the start. The spirit of thoroughness combined with daring is the mainspring of action in all military forces.

Israel's Army in Sinai is a case study in how group power is generated by consummate daring in the command. To the limit possible, leaders looked to their own forces, kept check on the sufficiency of supply, sought all information which might be helpful and exercised steady control over the whole. But when forces seemed too few, supply drained low and intelligence of the enemy was lacking, they still marched forward.

2...Lost Brigade

C OL. ARIEL SHARON, Israel Army, is a rolypoly para-
trooper who would be considered 'way overweight by the
United States' services.

Thrice wounded in the service of his country, extraordinarily
amiable in disposition, he is in manner almost boyishly shy.

Sharon's Brigade was given the most desperate gamble
among the many risks which composed the Sinai campaign.
It was the first force to be committed. On whether it fared
well or badly could pivot High Command decision about
whether to wage full-scale war against Egyptian Sinai or limit
operations to a raid by this one brigade.

Its mission taxed human energy to its limits and over an
incredibly prolonged period required repeatedly bold, clear
decisions by the commander amid utmost pressure. In these
things lies the value of the experience as a military document.
It is a shining example of prodigious performance by many
men because one man wills it.

D-Day for Sharon's Brigade was Monday, 29 October. Only
one of his paratroop battalions was to be air-dropped. Its
H-Hour was set at 1700. Dark would fall just thirty minutes
later.

The task of the brigade was to capture and hold the Mitla
Pass and the crossroads at Nakhl. At Mitla one roadblock
can hold back any deployment of Egyptian troops from the

port of Suez into eastern Sinai. Nakhl village was the training base of the fedayeen who had been terrorizing the frontier settlements in the Negev. The extermination of this base was cited as the main object for loosing Sharon's Brigade, irrespective of other developments. If the raid expanded into a war, Sharon's further task was to keep open the Kuntilla-Themed-Nakhl-Mitla axis for the passage of other troops.

At 1600, just one hour before the air-borne battalion was to drop on Mitla, the advance guard of Sharon's main column was to cross the frontier into Egyptian Sinai, bound for the same target.

Besides the one infantry battalion and its organic equipment, the Mitla Pass drop would include four antitank guns, two 120 mm mortars and eight jeeps for reconnaissance.

Under Sharon were four battalions including one battalion of artillery, using 25-pounders, and one battalion of heavy mortars. Two half-track companies were attached to carry the infantry. Also with the overland force were one light tank company using French AMX's, a surgical team, an airstrip team, three forward radio teams for dealing with the Air Force and two Piper Cubs. The light planes were to be used as jacks-of-all-trades.

For support, the brigade had one supply-dropping unit, a squadron of Dakotas. Fighter squadrons were supposed to protect the movement as much as possible, but Sharon was warned that their availability would not be constant because of requirements elsewhere.

From Israel's frontier to Mitla Pass, where the linkup was to take place, the distance overland is 156 miles. But all of these are excruciatingly hard miles and most of the way there is no road. The only pavement in the area runs between Mitla and Suez.

Never having seen the country, Sharon looked at the maps

and air photos and estimated to High Command that the brigade could go the distance in twenty-four hours. It was an excessively hopeful calculation.

Mitla Pass, proper, is no place for an air drop. It is a narrow pass between ranges, the peaks of which run to 870 yards. Its clifflike sides are but fifty to eighty yards apart. So the dropped battalion was to land fifteen miles to the east at a place called Colonel Parker's Memorial. With it would be dropped enough water, food and ammunition to stay the force twenty-four hours. Three days later, given time for the marking of the drop zones, supporting weapons would be dropped, with basic supply for another twenty-four hours.

About reserve enemy strength, it was known that one Egyptian brigade was based on Shalufa, near Suez, west of the Canal.

At Nakhl—the supply base for southeast Sinai—Sharon expected to find a battalion headquarters and two companies of infantry. Northward, on the road to Bir Hasne, was a company position. South of Nakhl was another company position. Between the two was a vehicle park. Reading the air photo, Sharon counted fifty vehicles in it.

At Kuntilla the enemy had one infantry platoon. In positions on the fortified cliffs above Themed were two more Egyptian infantry companies. Their park contained thirty vehicles. Flanking the road, after it passed through a notch in the cliff wall eight miles west of Themed, the bunker-and-trench system ran to a depth of two thousand yards. All of the perimeters within it were doubly fenced with barbed wire, which meant that they were mined.

Within Themed village itself was another enemy platoon. Themed lies fifty-one miles beyond Israel's frontier. More than the fortified positions there and the firepower to defend them, the dominant terrain feature beyond Themed made it

a formidable obstacle. There the great wadi is walled by a
north-south running cliff which cannot be outflanked. The
fortified notch is the only pass-through and one must go at it
head-on.

Kuntilla is only eight miles from the Israel border. But
there is no straight-line approach. Where the nearest road in
Israel ends, Kuntilla is thirty-six miles away. The area between
is either sand hill or wadi. Ancient caravan tracks thread this
wasteland, but they have not been used for any military purpose since World War I, when camels and horses found it
a trial.

The passage of three or four trucks will break down such
support as these desert tracks momentarily afford. With difficulty, today's average military supply vehicle can get through
the sand hills but can't take the wadis under its own power.

Themed itself is in a wadi and from there the track stays in
the wadi most of the way back to Kuntilla. Between the designated jump-off point in the Negev and Kuntilla there is neither
road nor track.

All of these natural considerations bore upon how Sharon
organized his force. He heavily weighted his advance guard,
putting in it one infantry battalion, two platoons of AMX's
and two batteries of artillery. The main body was to be
organized also as a combat team, with more infantry but fewer
heavy support weapons.

Sharon proposed to take both Kuntilla and Themed with
his advance guard, which tasks he reckoned would pretty well
sap its people of combat vigor. Thereafter, this van would
bypass Nakhl and roll on to Parker's Memorial as fast as possible. After capturing Nakhl, the combat team of the main
body would hold it with one company, having dropped off
another company to garrison Themed. All else in the column

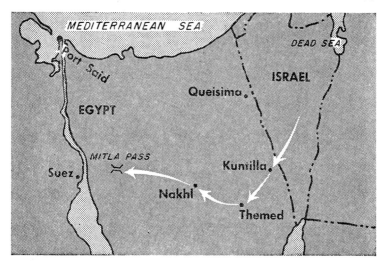

SHARON'S MARCH

was to close up on the advance guard, if possible, and help establish the brigade position east of Mitla.

Such was the general plan as Sharon devised it shortly after being told his task. There was no dwelling on alternatives or the problem of extrication if things went wrong. The brigade, minus the battalion which was to go air-borne, was supposed to be concentrated at the Negev settlement Ein-Hotsev by 1700 on 28 October, just twenty-four hours before H-Hour.

For the movement from Ein-Hotsev, it would have sixty miles of fair road, and beyond that forty miles of track, or of bumping over unmarked desert, before hitting its closest target.

Sharon calculated he would be ready to march by about 0300 hours on 29 October. While the dark lasted, the brigade would just barge ahead in closed column. There would be no chance for concealment in any case as the country is shrubless and wide open. However, ten miles east of the border was a heavily eroded sand-hill formation which would give the brigade some cover. The column could refuel there and make the final plunge during daylight. This last leg of the approach was certain to be a trial. But Sharon felt that between towing and winching, he could maintain the schedule.

Nothing quite worked out as planned. By nightfall on 28 October, most of the brigade had gathered at Ein-Hotsev. But the night wore on, and one convoy of six-by-six trucks needed to keep the brigade whole during the desert march still did not show.

At 0700, having lost four hours, Sharon decided he could wait no longer. One battalion was forthwith mounted on such civilian lorries as could be rounded up. The rest of the brigade was upon half-tracks and military trucks—well, not quite. One battery of antiaircraft had to be left behind for lack of vehicles. Also pared off for the same reason was the brigade's platoon of engineers. "Leave the men but take along the bull-dozer," said Sharon in an inspired moment.

So the start was made in broad daylight. Again changing plans, the column refueled while on the main road, forty miles from the border. It was a first, happy experiment with this technique. By doing it on the run, while the roadway was still smooth, the brigade had recovered possibly two of the lost hours. It still wasn't enough to afford the column any pause whatever during the worst part of the journey. The point crossed the border at 1600 and one hour later led part of the advance guard into Kuntilla.

This was the target—a village extending about 400 yards across the flat top of a conspicuous mesa which rose, sharp-sided, 450 feet above the surrounding desert. At either end of the village, covering the one road which exited to the west-ward, was a rock-walled watchtower with fire-slotted sides. Next to the mesa, on the north side, was a Bedouin well by which the village survived.

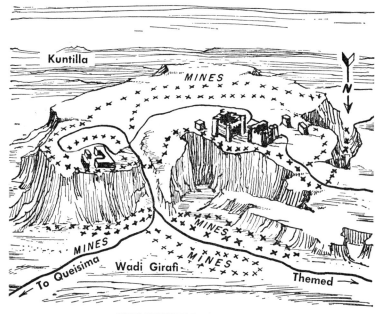

THE KUNTILLA POSITION

One reconnoitering Piper Cub reported to Sharon, as the lead vehicles rushed toward the mesa, that the Egyptians were running to man the towers and the nearby trenches. But none of his people had waited to see. The van whipped around the hill and moved straight in against the westward tower so that the attackers would have their backs to the setting sun. Its glare in the eyes of the defender was the only supporting fire used.

There was no cessation of motion until the eastern tower was also silenced. All resistance then ended. Sharon had lost one man wounded. One jeep and two of his half-tracks were disabled by mines.

But as he took the score and looked eastward across the desert, while the last light flickered, he also realized suddenly that he had lost the advance guard artillery and the main body of the brigade. The desert was empty. No following vehicle was anywhere in sight. For the time being, he did not know what had happened, later he learned: the sand had proved too deep. Every artillery piece had become stuck and all but one mortar truck. Two tanks and three half-tracks were also caught. Both fuel tankers—one for the tanks and the other for the half-tracks—were in the same situation. His first combat team was only partly accounted for; his second was nowhere that he knew.

To sum up, fifty vehicles could no longer move, and those which were still free could not get past the block. Sharon didn't know where his most important vehicles were or how to find them. As the dark closed down, all he could be sure of was the small force atop the Kuntilla mesa. An immobilized brigade was strung out for an unknown distance behind him.

Still, he decided to press on with what he had and with very little pause. Later, before he got rolling again, some inkling of the situation came to him by radio from the artillery commander. Sharon directed him to take over the job of freeing the stalled vehicles and closing the gap. Junior leaders were already at work. They had unloaded the one bulldozer and were using it to pull other machines out of the sand stretches.

At the same time Sharon radioed High Command, asking for an air drop of fuel for the tanks and of spare tracks for the vehicles which had thrown theirs in the sand. He said, "Get it ready and I'll tell you where to drop it later."

The reason for the decision to advance on Themed, irrespective of the beaching of the main body, was that Sharon viewed the fortified cliff as his worst obstacle and had determined to overcome it before the position could be reinforced. With the taking of Kuntilla, chance for further surprise in Sinai had been lost. Despite the depleting of his force, mobility for the moment seemed to outweigh concentration. One consideration gave him pause: he wasn't sure that he had enough fuel to stretch the distance.

At 2240 hours one lorry loaded with gasoline, towed by a half-track, pulled into Kuntilla. That did it. By then, most of the advance guard, his brigade headquarters and several platoons from his second infantry battalion were at hand and under control. Sharon ordered all present to get moving. He'd worry about the rest of the brigade when it caught up.

At 0345 on 30 October the point started its run through Themed village. The entrenched enemy platoon fired as the advance guard barreled through. From the careening vehicles Sharon's men returned fire, but none stopped to mop up.

At 0400 Sharon ordered the advance guard commander to attack the fortified cliff west of Themed without waiting for artillery support, the guns still being far behind.

He said, "However, wait until 0545. Then you'll get the rising sun. Those fellows up there will be looking straight into it. Maybe it's not as good as a barrage but it's the best we've got."

Since the attack would have to be a drive in column straight up the notch in the cliffside, the light tanks would have to lead the way.

Except for the armor and infantry, the rest of the force was told to disperse, dig in, conceal vehicles and be prepared for an enemy air strike. Also, via the Piper Cub relay, Sharon was hearing from the commander of the dropped battalion that he was on target, with thirteen men injured in the drop. His resupply had come in. He said he had shot up numerous enemy vehicles and captured a water tanker driving eastward from Mitla Pass.

As first light broke, it was clear that the Egyptians were already alerted. The cliff top buzzed with activity. The front of

Sharon's force was at least eighteen hundred yards east of the forward enemy pits along the skyline. But the Egyptian machine guns and mortars were firing all out, though at that range they could do no hurt.

Watching this futile display, Sharon decided on the spur of the moment to try to mystify the Egyptians with the novelty of his attack.

This was the plan: the half-tracks followed by the tanks would ride in column up the road toward the cliff until reaching the point where the "bullet swarm" really thickened. Then all vehicles would deploy in line astride the road with the armor on the right. The tanks would concentrate their fire against the enemy pits of the opposite flank; that way, because of perspective, they had a better chance of hitting pay targets.

Then after firing for about ten minutes, the tanks would dash to within 350 yards of the mine fields covering the enemy front. There, they would lay a smoke screen, dropping smoke canisters just in front of their own hulls. That done, they would drop back just a few yards to get maneuver room, then converge on the road and charge upward through the notch in column, firing to both flanks as they came up and over the rim.

Sharon felt sure that the road itself had not been mined; the Egyptians are somewhat careless about such details. However, such was the narrowness of the road where it threaded this opening in the rock wall that if one well-placed round disabled one lead vehicle the whole column would be blocked. There was the supreme but unavoidable risk.

The van of the column was still almost one mile short of the cliff when .50 caliber machine-gun fire began bouncing off its metal. Still, the force deployed, fired, smoked, regathered and charged exactly as planned.

When the AMX's topped the rise and charged past the

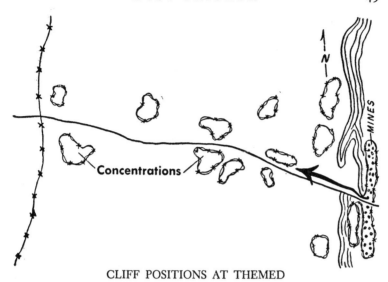

CLIFF POSITIONS AT THEMED

strongest enemy perimeter at the cliff front and leftward of
the road, all guns going, though no tank slowed to give the
redoubt searching fire, the whole enemy position from front
to rear—that is, this frontal resistance center and all the fortified parcels of ground behind it—collapsed.

In that charge, which was over before fear could dispel the
wild excitement of the ride, Sharon lost three dead and six
wounded. One half-track was disabled by a mine. Otherwise
the brigade remained sound. The enemy lost fifty killed,
fifteen prisoners and eleven lightly wounded. The other defenders ran away and Sharon's men did not try to pursue
them.

Time, by Sharon's initial estimate, had already run out. The
brigade had been on the road twenty-four hours and Mitla
Pass was still far distant. Until now most of the moving and
all of the hitting had been done by the one skinned-down
combat team of the advance guard which had lost its artillery.

Its men were wearing down; what reserve of energy they still possessed was hard to estimate. Sharon saw some of them dozing in the half-tracks before the battle smoke had cleared from the cliffs above Themed.

While that worried him, in the postdawn hour he could postpone for a little time decision on whether to press on once again with greatly tired troops, or rest them and await the main body. One imperative task permitted a respite. The dead and the wounded had to be evacuated to Themed village, whence the emergency cases could be flown out by Piper Cub.

So for an hour or so, the brigade halted in place while the work proceeded. During the interval Sharon moved about among his troops trying to measure the pulse beat. A few were fast asleep, curled up like kittens. Others were drooping but appeared too nervously tensed for rest. Still Sharon decided tentatively that the force had stayed strong enough to go on and take Nakhl. One reason for his optimism was that he personally felt keyed up by the easy success in the attack upward from the wadi, though he had been on his feet for fifty-two hours running.

The airstrip team had gone to work near Themed village. The Egyptian platoon had decamped. On the road to Themed, near midnight, Sharon had asked High Command to drop his resupply at that point soon after first light. The drop arrived at 0700. By then the Pipers were already using the strip to fly out the wounded.

His confidence rose on seeing these operations go smoothly. No word had come that the dropped battalion was in any real danger; so he felt no sweat. But he thought it best to hit the road as promptly as the work detail was completed. The inner voice said, "To win quickly you must keep going."

Amid this quiet, his reflections on decision ended abruptly.

Suddenly six MiG's swept in, coming low over the horizon and catching the brigade sprawled. They strafed and bombed the column in pairs, making three passes. When at last they pulled off, there were six more Israeli wounded to be evacuated.

Out of all proportion to this hurt was the moral impact on the camp. The attack had come while vehicles were being refueled. Sharon again moved about, looking at his men. Now they were going about their work haltingly, and frequently had to spell one another on relatively light tasks.

Seeing it, Sharon switched his decision. He passed the order, "Everybody rest." The advance guard would wait atop the cliff for the arrival of the main body. That change was made about 0830. On its heels, an observer in a Piper Cub radioed Sharon: "The field artillery battalion and the lorried infantry are already on the road and just leaving Kuntilla." So he knew he was right. Within three hours, the brigade would be made solid again.

By 1100 hours the camp seemed to be freshening; it astonished Sharon that seemingly exhausted troops could bound back so quickly.

First up, then down. Four Egyptian Vampires came in low, made two more passes and hit six more men. They seemed to get away scot-free. (See Appendix II, The Air Battle.) It didn't help that by radio, amid the strafing, Sharon got the reassuring information that his own Air Force would be ready to protect the column soon after 1300.

To move or stay was again the question. Decision was forced by the return of a Piper Cub which Sharon had sent west to look over the scene at Parker's Memorial. From air to ground, came the relayed message: "We are being shelled by heavy mortars and have taken two air strikes." It had the postscript that the strike had demolished the dropped bat-

talion's only Piper while evacuating wounded. Then came
another message from the Piper overhead: "There is evi-
dence of an enemy advance from Suez."

That did it. Again Sharon reversed decision. The advance
guard must push on, not to bypass Nakhl but to attack it.

Ordered at 1200 hours, the advance began at exactly 1245.
By comparison with what had been, the west-running road
was a boulevard. The advance guard sped along. It was fifty
miles to Nakhl. There were frequent encounters with enemy
half-tracks and armed trucks; they were finished off without
stopping. By 1630 Sharon was within machine-gun range
of the village.

He had asked High Command to ready an air strike against
Nakhl and lay it on before he got there. By sheer chance the
jets arrived above the column just as it drove to within
sight of the mud huts. Though the evening was not really
cloudy, there was a thick overcast and the sky already was
darkening. Sharon was on his radio talking to the jets. Their
commander said, "We can't see Nakhl at all and can hardly
see you."

Sharon realized nothing could be done about it. Between
the overcast and the blending of the mud houses with the
desert flat, the target had become invisible from above. There
was no use wasting fuel in vain orbiting when he had a better idea. So he told the air commander, "Contact the force at
Parker's Memorial and get permission to interdict enemy
movement from Suez." The jets were less than ten minutes
from the dropped battalion: the advance guard was still
four hours away.

This switch may sound foolish since dark was falling fast.
But it was a question of topography. At Nakhl everything
looked the same from the air. Between Suez and the Mitla
Pass the road was a slot between hills and couldn't be missed.

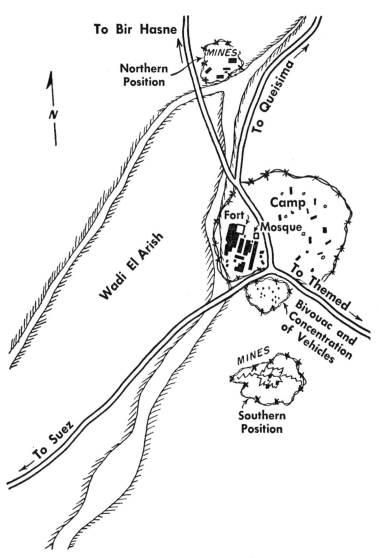

NAKHL AND ITS DEFENSES

Two minutes were lost in making the decision. Nakhl was still fifteen hundred yards distant. Sharon issued the order which was passed down to the companies: "Be ready to attack in fifteen minutes."

Then came the unexpected break which fired up all hands. Out of the dusk came driving one of the lost artillery batteries. Its guns were laid in five minutes, and with eight minutes to go, they opened fire. As the first round got away, another battery arrived. It opened fire with five minutes to go. Between them, the two batteries bracketed the town, hitting into the fortifications at both ends of it.

At 1645 the advance guard went "galloping" straight in. In the attack were two under-strength infantry companies on half-tracks, one on lorries and one platoon of AMX light tanks. Half of the tanks and one rifle company were to go against the position at the far end of the village. The lorried company was to ride 750 yards, then dismount and attack the nearest position on foot. The others were to stand by.

Already the last rays of day were shining directly in Sharon's eyes. It would be dark by the time his troops closed. He couldn't take the chance of ranging in more artillery as it came up. He couldn't use tanks with the infantry line moving afoot, because in the dark it would breed confusion. Dusk is even more deceitful than pitch-black.

That attack, so hastily contrived, went as planned. Before its line closed, men could see the Egyptians running from their positions. The shellfire seemed to "bounce them right out of the ground." The artillery sustained fire until the Israeli infantry was "right on top of the target."

Sharon could no longer see what was doing. Confident that the battalion commander had everything under control and the attack would not falter, Sharon tuned in on the enemy radio chatter, not to play it cool, but feeling he might learn something.

What he heard was sheer panic talk. The Egyptians in the Nakhl headquarters were quoting their own air observers. The far-strung-out state of the brigade, which had been raising a towering dust cloud for thirty-five miles back, gave them the impression that a mighty host was advancing. There was at least this dividend from the brigade's floundering.

Utter demoralization resulted; no Egyptian tried to fight. Sharon's force captured Nakhl intact without losing a man. The enemy lost seven dead, all killed by artillery. The others ran. Next day the enemy survivors collected in the wadi and counterattacked. They perished foolishly, fifty-one being killed and twenty-five becoming prisoners, without drawing blood from the defenders. How many got away across the desert is unknown.

In Nakhl the brigade found military workshops, heavy stores of ammunition and food and a sufficient arsenal to indicate that about five hundred men had based there for training. But there were no fedayeen; a large supply of their distinctive caps was the only token of their connection with Nakhl.

At Nakhl, Sharon concluded the first fighting round of Israel Army's Sinai campaign. Thus far only one other blow had landed anywhere else around the border. And it was a preventive move intended to seal off one line of advance against Sharon's overextended brigade. What later became a war was hence limited at the moment to this one large-scale raid.

Where Sharon stood, despite his success, he was still highly vulnerable. No friendly force intervened between his flank and the main weight of the Egyptian field army directly northward. There was enough enemy armor within three hours' ride of his scattered command to pulverize it.

We must, therefore, leave Sharon's Brigade at Nakhl for a while in order to view the concurrent developments elsewhere. Along the border ridges there was much motion but thus far little fighting. If the High Command in this initial period looked for a sign that its war machine was well oiled and clicking, it sought in vain. The events of the first twenty-four hours had proved only that the high spirit of the Army was equal to the venture while saying nothing about its material sufficiency for the task ahead.

3 ... Muddle Through

SELDOM has anything so venturesome started less promisingly. Rarely, if ever, in fighting operations has a probe across an enemy frontier supplied better argument for keeping risks limited instead of going pell-mell into a full-scale war.

All around the border, save at one spot, the field army remained on leash. After Sharon hit Kuntilla, the world heard the news that Israel was invading Sinai. Still in balance, however, was a possible High Command decision about whether to strike a full-armed blow against Egypt or downgrade the adventure to a retaliatory raid, pull back Sharon's Brigade after it had fumigated Nakhl, and stack arms.

That first night Colonel Sharon had become swallowed by the dark, and somewhere behind him his main body was stuck amid the sands. What fortune would attend that stroke, if Sharon could get his brigade collected, was for the time beyond prediction.

One other enterprise had been timed to support Sharon, whichever way the wind blew. During the first night, the brigade under Col. Josef Harpaz, whose nickname is "Yosh," was to seize the road junction at Queisima so that Sharon's sprawled-out column would not be wide open to attack from the north while halfway to Nakhl. The maneuver would not put a shield between the battalion at Parker's Memorial and the Egyptian armor around Bir Hamm; it would simply block one road.

But as the hour of main decision approached, Harpaz did not have his forces in hand. According to the situation reports, Harpaz was attacking. This, however, was a euphemism. Far-scattered and leg-weary, the elements of Harpaz's Brigade were moving haltingly toward their objective, beaten by the clock and buffeted by the country.

The benumbed start should have caused anxiety everywhere and thrown a chill into the higher levels. Among warriors, as the usual thing, if there is a possible choice between a soft option and a hard one, a smash hit in the opening round will steel decision. By the same token, what begins falteringly is best ended.

This night the brigade under Harpaz carried no such load on its shoulders. The brigade itself felt harassed by the unex-pected and almost insuperable difficulties of its movement by night through unknown country. But higher up there was no sweat. Almost nothing in the two opening maneuvers was proceeding according to plan. On the other hand, the plan was itself highly flexible and well cushioned.

Miracles were not expected of Harpaz; he expected to per-form none. Despite the fact that the brigade had been as-signed a key, opening mission, it had been weakly, unevenly vehicularized for its lunge into the untracked Negev and through the hilly wasteland along the Egyptian border.

That was not the consequence of miscalculation or last-minute improvisation. In fact, Harpaz was one of the first brigade commanders to be given his task. He had known what was coming some days before the others. Among them all, he at least had sufficient time to prepare his reservists for the undertaking.

Where the pinch came was that Israel's Army did not have enough half-tracks and cross-country fighting vehicles at hand to move all of the hitting forces. Harpaz's Brigade, which

would attack first in its part of Sinai, had to be content with
third-rate transportation. It was deprived so that the brigades
which would go the longer routes would be mounted for the
marathon.

In this decision there was elementary fair play and hard
tactical logic. The brigades which would strike deepest were
also expected to encounter the heaviest opposition in men,
weapons and strength of works.

Harpaz's mission was given to him in about these words:
"You will be ready to take the fortified hills in front of
Queisima. After, you will be ready to open the road to Abu
Agueila and explore toward Bir Hasne."

High Command reckoned that Harpaz and his men could
achieve that much by the seats of their pants, if need be.
There was only one Egyptian battalion deployed in the entrenchments of Hills 330 and 335 east of Queisima. The outposted village of Sabha just over the border was supposed to
hold not more than one platoon.

Harpaz agreed in this light estimate of the enemy after
looking at the air photos of Queisima. What impressed him
most was that the Egyptians had not taken main advantage
of the high ground but had fortified the two hills along the
first shelf just above the base. He said, "That's just the wrong
way to do it."

They got together, Harpaz and the brigade, on Friday
night, 26 October. One day earlier his soldiers had been
civilians making their accustomed rounds in the Tel Aviv
area. On assembling, many of them were meeting him for
the first time. They saw a small, ginger-haired man, age
thirty-three, who looks and talks like a Texas cowhand,
though he migrated from Poland to Palestine when a babe
in arms.

Harpaz is high-school educated, which is the average level

among Israel's higher commanders. What is most noticeable about this company is that they are acute listeners. A joker by nature, Harpaz concentrates so intensely that his face looks pained.

Upon summoning the men, he had but one more day in which to organize the brigade before it marched. For them, that meant assembling on Harpaz at his command post 135 miles to the south, drawing equipment and forming up. By the end of the day his brigade was at his elbow, 85 percent mobilized. Other men caught up while it was on the road. In the end only two missed the call altogether. Both were later investigated and cleared.

For this opening move by which the brigade formed on Harpaz, the commandeered transportation was good enough. The city buses and commercial vehicles rolled along easily enough over paved country roads.

But in the pause which followed, while the brigade awaited the "go" signal, nothing else arrived, except word that the task had been slightly modified. Instead of taking Sabha and both fortified hills on the first night, Harpaz was to wait until morning before attacking Hill 335 and the village of Queisima. High Command had begun to worry that the Egyptian air might react sharply.

Harpaz, on the other hand, was worried only that his transport couldn't get over the desert. So he had a thought. The three battalions and support weapons units were formed. He showed them the map of the border and pointed out the spot where the brigade would jump off. Then he said to his men, "Get to this place I have shown you—in your cars if you can make it—on foot if you can't—but get there!"

He thought it was a good pep talk, just the right thing to say. Later, he had second thoughts about it. There is always the danger of being taken too literally.

HILL 335 SEEN FROM QUEISIMA

On Saturday night, the advance began on a follow-the-leader basis. Still riding in its civilian buses and trucks, the brigade was not responsive to radio control along its length. The column was already fully in motion when at last ten half-tracks and twenty weapons carriers overtook and joined it.

That looked like a break, but for the time being they simply brought up the rear, running empty. Lack of road space and of radio control over movement dictated that arrangement. In this way, the city buses, which carried the advance guard, were compelled to break the trail.

No sooner did the van of the column veer westward from the Beersheba-Elat Highway than it was already in open desert, with the lead vehicle trying to follow an irregular caravan track through the sea of sand. It was an unequal contest. The buses bumped slowly forward as the men got out and pushed. But muscles grew weary swiftly, for most of the riders were city-bred soldiers. Between the darkness and the dunes, the column was soon brought to a standstill.

By sunrise the brigade was stuck solid and strung out over nearly five miles of trail space. Its van was still six miles short of the spot where it was to form for the attack. Harpaz was forward, mounted in a jeep, and therefore still mobile. He drove back along the stalled column. His thought was to get the half-tracks up and use them to extricate the buses. What he saw "made everything look black." The sand had tightened like a vise along the whole convoy.

When he rode forward again, leading the half-tracks, things were even worse. His words returned to haunt him. "Get to this place I have shown you!" The brigade had heard it as a peremptory order. Now some of the platoons were out trying to push the stalled vehicles. But in larger numbers they had already quit the column and were hiking across the desert toward the jump-off area. There was no way to recall them.

Leaving his second-in-command to organize the rescue act by the half-tracks and shepherd the stragglers, Harpaz rode for the rendezvous area forward. By noontime, approximately 70 percent of the brigade's call-up strength had there assembled around him, making it by-guess-and-by-God. Among the early arrivals were some who, getting their summons late, had hitchhiked down the Elat road and then marched singly across country. It was a tryout for Israel's only secret weapon —the unexampled fidelity of her reserve soldiers.

That afternoon, while his command remained far scattered, Harpaz wrote his plan for observation of the area. After sundown he sent out his first patrols. Their task was limited. They would study the approaches and identify the landmarks which would be useful to the attacking battalions.

Along this part of the frontier, the sand ridges on Israel's side run to three hundred yards high and form a natural screen.

The brigade was still on friendly soil. Harpaz reckoned, from what his patrols told him, that his whole operation remained undetected. There was not a sign of reaction from the Egyptian side.

Sabha is the closest settlement over the border. On Monday night, 29 October, Harpaz moved his command post onto Egyptian soil two miles northeast of Sabha. One infantry battalion went with him as did his reconnaissance unit, which was mounted on half-tracks.

His second battalion was still twelve miles distant inside Israel, jouncing along on the city buses, save when the riders unloaded to push. Their strength was running out even as time was running short.

Though H-Hour had been set at one hour past midnight, it afforded no prospect of surprise. Sharon's people had already hit Kuntilla and dropped at Parker's Memorial. It was therefore a reasonable assumption that the enemy camps were alerted all over Sinai.

By 0100 hours all of Harpaz's forces were supposed to be toeing the mark, coiled for a co-ordinated attack at the starting gun. The battalion right at hand would fall on Sabha. The battalion advancing on buses would go at the main target, engaging the fortified hills east of Queisima.

Harpaz's plan had been neatly drawn to keep casualties low and gather in the whole Egyptian position in one clutch without directly violating the High Command's last instruction.

The two ridges defending Queisima were in depth; that is to say that both straddled the main road leading to the village, with Hill 330 coming first.

Its works were probably garrisoned by the greater part of the enemy battalion. To move at them head-on would be foolhardy. The battalion would divide to form a pincers. From both ends of the ridge, six platoons would start toward each other moving at right angles to the way the entrenchments faced. Harpaz reckoned that the Egyptians would flee this enfilade before either of his own flanks ran into the other's fire.

Simultaneously, two other platoons would clamp onto the end of Hill 335 in much the same fashion, except that they would not converge. That would create a diversion and prevent 330's reinforcement. Still another group of fifteen of Harpaz's soldiers would set up a roadblock midway between the two ridges.

This was artful dodging in view of the High Command's stricture against assaulting Hill 330 prior to daylight lest an overextended force become punctured by air bombardment. Hill 330 would be squeezed, not attacked, certainly an ingenious distinction.

Harpaz's contempt for the Egyptian fortifications was based partly upon his high hopes for his own artillery performance. The air photos showed that the trenches and bunkers were well wired in, with the entanglements enclosing three separate mine fields, all running roughly parallel to the enemy front. So if his guns and mortars could zero in on the enemy earthworks, whatever fell short would clobber the line of obstacles, since the two were closely joined.

Early, this was a high expectation. Late, it dissolved under the harsh realities of supporting weapons management in a situation where nothing had been accurately measured or registered.

Within the artillery nothing went right except that there were guns enough. To the southeast of Harpaz, one battalion of 155 mm howitzers was setting up on Hill 450. Directly to his north, a battalion of 25-pounders had deployed off the road and signaled that it was ready to fire on order. Closer to hand, the 120 mm mortar platoon had finished digging its pits and now stood by.

Here was enough potential thunder, provided it could be loosed. That was something else again, as Harpaz learned while H-Hour rushed closer. Having at last gotten into position, the 155 mm battalion stayed silent, unable to raise either Harpaz or the advancing infantry battalion on its radio. Hearing nothing, Harpaz at last sweated. The big guns were less than three miles distant in a beeline, but to get to them, the only possible route ran a roundabout twelve miles, due to the ruggedness of the intervening country. It would be senseless to start a liaison officer out.

Harpaz could hear from the 25-pounder battalion. But what he heard was no good. "We haven't got the range to Hill 330; have you got the range?" Harpaz didn't have it. So it was pointless to deploy the battalion.

From the heavy-mortar platoon came the same cry. "What's the range to 330?" For lack of it, Harpaz told the mortars to make ready to support the attack on Sabha, the range of which was subject to an educated guess.

With one hour to go, he wrote off his heavy firepower as lost. The rush of events made it a minor disappointment. At midnight the battalion commander nudging Sabha radioed: "On position and ready." Then came the call from the battalion commander who was to attack Hill 330. He said, "I'm running hours behind schedule and I can't tell you why." Since Harpaz could guess why, he didn't give his subordinate hell. He said only, "Do your best." Hour by hour, his own difficulties had mounted because of the unanticipated obstacles to movement in a countryside which had seemed not too formidable according to the map descriptions. Now he could see, possibly a little too late, that his badly vehicularized key battalion may have been assigned a task that lay beyond its power. More irritating was the realization that he could do nothing to help it except withhold from putting needless pressure on the battalion commander.

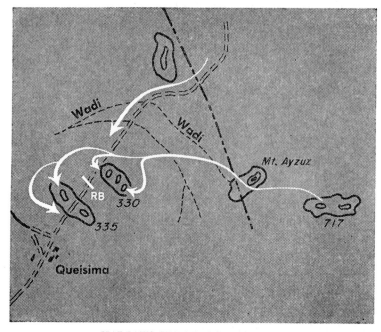

HARPAZ'S TWO-RIDGE ATTACK

This battalion's peculiar ordeal is best viewed through the eyes of its young commander. During the daylight hours he and his troops had made a forced march which had killed the greater part of eight hours. They had done this simply to get from their bivouac ground to their assembly area on the shoulder of Mount Ayzuz. The battalion was still mounted on its city buses. But such vehicles were never meant to travel over the wash-strewn, deeply eroded desert that lies southeast of the Jebel Tsabah. Much of the way, the vehicles had had to be pushed through deep sand; the men were physically worn before reaching the ground where they should have started completely fresh.

All unit commanders had preceded the main body by several hours so that they might get a view of the two target hills from the height of Mount Ayzuz while the light still held. But it was not a satisfactory reconnaissance. The sun was setting. Its rays half-blinded them. They could see Hills 330 and 335 in outline; their facings seemed to be precipitous and each looked more like a nest of small ridges than a solid hill mass. Of the middle ground between Israel's border and the objectives they saw little before the light faded.

Coming along under its seconds-in-command, the column finally closed on Mount Ayzuz at 2050, already four hours late. There they quit the buses, distributed radios and ammunition, and, in fact, went through the whole process of grouping and girding for the attack.

Hill 330 was supposed to be about nine and one-third miles beyond, all of it rough, unknown country which had to be traversed in darkness. With H-Hour set for 0100, this battalion would have needed wings to keep its assignment.

Still, it tried, only to discover that the reality was grimmer than the prospect. The actual distance was just under twelve miles—impossibly long for an approach march to battle even in flat country.

Starting down from the saddle of Mount Ayzuz, the column was checked first by the trench of a cliff-walled wadi which no one had known was there. It was a task for Alpinists, and the battalion lost ninety minutes clambering down the wall. By 2230 hours the commander had just reached the wadi bed. Scores of his men had flopped there from exhaustion.

He let them rest there a few minutes. Then his scouts lost their way, tried to follow the wadi course and led the battalion too far north. Already he had realized that his force couldn't keep its appointment and had radioed Harpaz, "You must let me have three more hours." But there was still another and another rock-walled tributary of the main wadi for his men to cross before they could ever enter upon flat ground, and they stumbled along as if nothing moved them but the instinct to escape the country.

Of their ordeal, Harpaz could see nothing. Still, he realized that it was time for decision. On his own, he determined to suspend H-Hour for so long as was needed to complete the array. Though High Command had set the hour and other movements in the unfolding plan were timed to it, the people up there would understand that no other sound course was possible.

Having notified the other units of the delay, Harpaz sent an officer with twelve pioneers to scout the trace which led from his own position into Queisima to make sure it was free of mines. For extra insurance, he wanted to be able to send the reconnaissance unit posthaste that way if its firepower was needed. At 0200 hours this mission reported, "The track is clear."

Right about then, the battalion commander nearest him radioed: "I think Sabha is deserted." Harpaz said, "Prowl into it but don't use any fire."

One hour later the battalion commander going to Hill 330 called, saying, "I'm still short of the objective but I can't tell you how far."

The bind was now tightening steadily. By 0530 hours the sky would be light. There had been time for the Egyptians to rush medium armor into Queisima. If a worn-down infantry battalion, without armor or artillery help, were to meet such a column on the road, it could hardly save itself, even by flight. Brooding on this possibility, Harpaz suddenly saw that with time running out, it no longer made sense to suspend the attack in all sectors, simply because forces weren't ready at the main point. He realized that if he could dispose of all other problems, he could then give single-minded attention to the fight forward in the hour when he would be most needed.

At 0300 hours he ordered his nearest battalion: "Take Sabha."

The artillery with the 25-pounders was forthwith displaced to ground directly east of that village.

The reconnaissance unit was advanced to the border, whence its half-tracks could quickly move on Queisima.

Then he called High Command and said, "Release to me a company of light tanks [AMX's]; I'll need them here by morning." It was agreed.

At 0330 hours his luck changed—just a little. Via a relay through a support unit in the rear, the battalion commander of the 155's at last made radio contact with him. He was told: "Stand ready."

At 0400 hours came the call from the commander of the lost battalion. "I'm next Hill 330: we're ready to go: I want artillery."

Easily said, hard done. The 155's had the bearing but they didn't have the range. Harpaz said, "Fire anyway."

They did. But it was impossible to follow the bursts either from the battery positions or from where the infantry crouched next to the enemy hill. Harpaz ordered the guns to suspend fire, which meant that his infantry must assault unsupported.

He didn't have to tell them. At 0430 hours the commander assaulting Hill 330 radioed him: "We've got part of their works. But there's heavy automatic fire sweeping the slope. I judge they still have one strong point farther up the hill."

Asked Harpaz, "How about the platoons sent against Hill 335?"

He said, "I don't know; I'm not able to get in touch with them."

Convinced that things were "beginning to look really good," Harpaz sent the reconnaissance group barreling down the track toward Queisima, with lights full on, to help the fight at Hill 330 "in any way possible."

There followed one of those informational voids amid crisis which ever fray a commander's nerve. For thirty-five minutes not a word came from Hill 330. Having taken off, the reccy unit failed to report progress. Nothing came from the battalion attacking Sabha. His own guns being silent, Harpaz was in the odd situation of commanding in a battle without hearing a friendly voice or a shot.

So at 0500 hours he got in his own half-track and rode as hard as he could go for Hill 330. Arrived at its base a half-hour later, he again heard the voice of the battalion commander over radio: "This whole hill's in my hands. I'm on top of it. I've lost two killed and twelve wounded. But we're all right. About Hill 335, I can't tell you. I've heard nothing."

There had been approximately ninety Egyptian soldiers on Hill 330. Though they had not fought too well, they had gotten three Alpha machine guns, three 62 mm mortars and some rifles into action on the local ground, along with covering fire provided by a battery of 81 mm mortars based on Queisima village. There were a dozen or so machine-gun-armed jeeps along a trail leading down from the hill. These were not used to build up the defending fire; but when the attacking fire pressed close, the survivors of the Egyptian garrison mounted their chariots and fled.

The battalion commander who had taken Hill 330 just then ran his own jeep onto a shu-mine which blew off a tire and wheel. But while repairs were being made, he was already on radio trying to get Harpaz. He wanted permission to move his main force to Hill 335. The fight was over on Hill 330.

Harpaz was already on wing and didn't get the message. Daylight was now coming fast. Without stopping for a second look at Hill 330, Harpaz was riding for Hill 335.

He got there shortly after 0600 hours and promptly bumped into the reconnaissance group. Its half-tracks had barely

paused at Hill 330; the fight there seemed to be won. They
were now idling east of Hill 335 in what should have been
the Egyptian field of fire. But the field was silent.

At its crest, Hill 335 was shrouded in mist. Occasionally
the wind wafted it aside and men could be seen moving along
the skyline. They looked to Harpaz like his own soldiers. But
he couldn't be sure. The distance was too great for shouting
and he heard nothing on radio.

He said to the officer commanding the half-tracks, "Get to
the other side of the hill; deploy along one flank and wait."

It was completed in the nick of time, this movement. Suddenly fire beat against the ridge top—the fire of several machine guns—and the few men up there flattened.

Out of the heavy mist which draped the rear of Hill 335
came charging one and one-half companies of Egyptian infantry. Harpaz couldn't see it, but the reccy half-tracks were
set just right to enfilade this line as it closed on the lower slope
in counterattack.

The Egyptians were unaware of the trap, due to the covering
mist. The machine guns on the six half-tracks opened fire
together. It was over in about twenty minutes, the enemy
force destroyed in total, the reccy unit losing a half-dozen
men wounded.

There was one mile to go into Queisima. Leading the reccy
unit, Harpaz headed for the houses. Briefly, there was a brisk
trading of fire, none of it organized as to the other side, none
of it doing hurt. By 0720 hours he had the village. Nothing
remained but to round up such Egyptians as had fled to the
houses and disarm them. The team of armor which had been
rushed to Harpaz from an upcoming brigade that was to extend the attack over the same axis had meanwhile arrived in
time to help conclude the action.

The prize, as to the village itself, wasn't much. Queisima

could be—and once was—the center of a flourishing agrarian civilization. Less than one league from it is the great artesian spring of Ein-Qudeirat, the Kadesh Barnea of Bible times, where the People stayed thirty-eight years. Now, as when Moses drank there, enough water bubbles upward from the rocks to supply the needs of an army corps. There are a dozen or so houses at the Queisima crossroads pleasantly shaded by palms. No one had lived there for years but the Egyptian military garrison.

During this day the other brigade under Col. Uri Ben-Ari, which was to pass through Harpaz, moved from El Auja to a new assembly area near Queisima. By design, at the beginning Ben-Ari's armor had been given a utilitarian role and its power would be used according to the way the battle developed, whether to take Queisima if Harpaz faltered, drive for Mitla Pass if Sharon failed, advance on El Arish if the attack along the coast stalled, or strike toward Egypt the short way over the old Roman road running to Ismailia.

These four options were already cut to two by the fighting of the first night. Harpaz was sitting on his objective and Sharon was well on his way, highly mobile if not ideally unified. Despite the attenuation of Sharon's Brigade, its up-front velocity was so impressive that High Command wasn't fretting about operations in the south.

Late in the afternoon, Harpaz sent his reccy company and one platoon of the AMX's down the road to Nakhl, sixty or so miles away. Sharon's Brigade had not yet mopped up that part of the desert. But getting to Sharon was part of the task.

4...Short of Mitla

HAVING gained Nakhl and lost nothing doing it, Sharon for the first time felt disquieted.

He knew that Ben-Ari's armor was parked around Queisima. But he reckoned that it should have moved on southwestward to Bir Hasne. Standing on that road juncture, it would be between him and the main body of the Egyptian armor which was basing around Bir Gifgafa and Bir Hamm. At Nakhl he was already out on a limb and could almost hear the wood cracking. Every mile that he moved westward toward Mitla Pass would put him closer to the Egyptian armor and farther away from Ben-Ari's tanks, which were already heavily disadvantaged in point of distance.

But there was no help for it now. At Themed he had dropped two infantry companies for lack of sufficient vehicles to move at the desired speed. At Nakhl he pared off two more infantry companies, one artillery battery and two mortar batteries, to be sure of holding the place.

His brigade, as it mounted up to ride west, counted six rifle companies, formed into two battalions, two artillery batteries and one mortar battery.

His radio began to buzz. The Piper was up there somewhere in the night relaying this message from the dropped battalion: "Our surgeon has been badly wounded during an air strike."

Then came a second message: "Enemy attacks against us

have ceased as a result of the jet strike which you sent against the road."

That gave him tremendous satisfaction. He radioed back: "Tell the command that Brigade will reach there in four hours."

At 1930 hours, 30 October, the column started moving. At 2230 it closed on the armed camp at Parker's Memorial. The road had been comparatively smooth. The night was quiet.

PARATROOP OBJECTIVE: PARKER'S MEMORIAL

The dropped battalion's perimeter had been rigged for all-around defense. Some of the mines and wire had to be lifted to form a lane so that the brigade could enter the enclosure. But there was more than that. Above the entrance, some welcoming committee had hoisted a freshly painted sign:

INTERNATIONAL BOUNDARY
SHOW YOUR PASSPORTS

By then Sharon's men had been moving and fighting for thirty-nine hours since leaving Ein-Hotsev. Sharon read the sign and thought it a wonderful jest. But as his troops filed through he noticed that not a man laughed. At last the thought struck him forcefully: "My brigade is physically spent."

Still, he felt fairly good, though he hadn't closed his eyes in seventy hours. Maybe that was because he had been up front in the column where the dust, and consequently the fatigue, are less.

At 2300 hours, after getting a full account from the local commander, he called a conference of all commanders to issue orders for the reorganization of the expanded camp and for the movement to capture Mitla Pass.

He intended to tell the others that the brigade would again carry on, starting at 0400 hours. That would put the advance guard at the entrance to the pass, ready to engage, when first light broke. He reckoned that five hours' sleep would be more than enough to freshen the men in these circumstances.

But he couldn't get the words out. As he opened his mouth to speak, he looked at his officers who sat facing him in a semi-circle. Every one of them was sound asleep. The sight narcotized him. His tongue thickened, the sounds choked in his throat, he fell flat and was almost instantly asleep.

Nature had taken over because Sharon, an acute judge of the physical powers of other men, had for once pushed himself beyond sensible limits. Many a general has been stripped of his battle command for making the same error. In Sharon's case, it wasn't fatal.

He slept for four hours and fifteen minutes. It might have been longer had not an air drop come in over the camp and landed one 600-pound bundle within three feet of Sharon's head. That wakened him and reconvened the conference.

The nighttime drop fell directly on the bivouac area, fortunately without hitting a man, though there were many near misses. It was partly Sharon's fault.

Originally, it was planned to supply the dropped battalion wholly by air, while the rest of the brigade's requirements would be trucked in. The trials of the road had convinced Sharon this was impossible. So from Nakhl forward he kept radioing High Command that the whole force at Parker's would have to be air-supplied. High Command took him at his word and moved too fast.

While he had slept, a message arrived saying, "You will get your air strike in the morning." Being thoughtful people, his message-center crew had tried gently to arouse him and then given it up as a bad job. Now, a little belatedly, he read it to his officers and said, "So let's get moving."

His finger pointed directly at a cherub-faced, twenty-six-year-old battalion commander, Maj. Modecai Gur, who had led the fight at Nakhl and ridden with the van all the way. Again he was drawing the same assignment. His battalion was to mount up immediately and head for the pass. The others would follow.

He got the order at 0400 hours. By 0430, his battalion was already one mile on the road and wheeling toward the pass as fast as it could travel. Gur had decided that his main chance lay in threading the defile as first light touched the peaks, leaving the bottom of the canyon still dark.

But Gur had not been gone ten minutes when a one-word order reached Sharon by radio: "Stop!" Slightly baffled, he relayed it to Gur, and the whole movement halted. No explanation followed. Sharon guessed that the field army as a whole had become overextended and there wasn't sufficient air cover to make the spread.

Turned about, the brigade immediately dispersed all vehicles. There was almost no natural cover, and such rocks and ledges as might have helped them were cloaked in ground fog. But at least they scattered.

No sooner was the process completed than four Vampire jets roared toward the brigade from the direction of Suez. Directly overhead, they were engaged by two Israeli Meteors. Two Vampires were shot down and the other two ran.

Sharon saw almost nothing of these duels, not because of the fog but because he was head down, digging a foxhole. But his radio was at hand and he was hearing the blow-by-blow story from his own observation posts. One reported that a third Vampire was burning as it got away. It spoke truly. Later in the day the bailed-out pilot was made a prisoner.

While the sky brightened and the brigade marked time, Sharon reconnoitered the general position. The quick look convinced him that what had served the dropped battalion well enough for forty hours was no longer safe for the brigade, now that the Sinai campaign was for total stakes.

That wasn't the problem. Sharon was stewing again about the open door at Bir Hasne and what would happen if he had suddenly to engage a full brigade of medium T-34's with a half-dozen light tanks on flat ground.

Warning had come to him by radio that the Egyptian brigade at Bir Gifgafa was headed his way. It might be a false alarm. But if the enemy armor could move directly south via the great wadi which ran almost directly from its base to Parker's Memorial, it was already virtually knocking at his back door. The distance was about thirty-six miles. Sharon didn't believe Egyptians would be that venturesome, but then he couldn't be sure.

It was still a beautiful argument for resuming his own forward movement. There were steep-sided, rock-crowned foothills on either side of the road just short of the pass. Nested on this high ground, the brigade might be made shockproof.

All tactical logic has a utilitarian ambivalence which works to the advantage of the imaginative commander on the spot, as in Sharon's case. If he wishes sufficiently to resume an offensive enterprise, he can almost invariably find a defensive reason for so doing.

The more Sharon reflected, the more urgent the move seemed. He so told the Southern Command on radio and asked its permission to advance to the foothill line.

At 1100 hours its Chief of Staff arrived by Piper Cub. Sharon gave him the argument. He looked the ground over and told Sharon to proceed "provided you don't get involved in any big battles." During operations, such strictures are habitual with Israel's General Staff. Move but try not to get hurt; it is another way of saying that man is the least expendable value in an army.

Sharon felt no qualms whatever on this score. His Pipers had reported to him: "We see little or no signs of enemy troops in the pass." Patrols had gone forward and returned without drawing a shot. To Sharon's eye, the heights looked empty except for his own observation posts on the foothills.

But considering what had been told him, he decided not to risk the force as a whole. To facilitate the movement to the foothills, he'd set up a task force to reconnoiter Mitla Pass as a preliminary. Of course he was fudging a bit; otherwise the tale would have been shorter.

Being already set up to westward of the brigade, Gur drew the assignment. His view of the situation is best understood by returning to the close-up view of the false start made earlier in the morning.

Gur, like Sharon, is a fighting optimist. Unlike Sharon he is college-educated, and might have been a scientist except that he preferred paratrooping.

5 ... Ambush

GUR'S column started with a rush and stopped the same way. For his part, he would have kept the column barreling straight toward Suez. Four hours of sleep had refreshed him and he felt no caution; such was the consequence of the brigade's push-over victories earlier.

But he was not more than a mile on the road when Sharon radioed him: "Hold it! We've got an order not to enter the pass." High Command had intervened at just the right moment to keep the battalion from threading the defile under cover of dark. Feeling that his best chance was gone, Gur back-pedaled six miles to get his vehicles out of flat desert and into a shrub-strewn ravine lest there be an enemy air strike.

There, until the sun was high, he awaited the decision. The men slept. Finally Sharon came to him and said, "We're satisfied the pass is clear of Egyptians. You are not going into an operation. This is a recon. If you meet heavy fire turn back. We don't want casualties at this stage."

Almost as an afterthought, Sharon added that his deputy, Lieut. Col. Ytzhak Hossi, would accompany the force. That still left Gur boss man. He reflected cheerfully, "I guess he wants a nice ride to the Canal."

Still, as Sharon apportioned its forces, this column was loaded for bear. Besides Gur's two best rifle companies, which were mounted in half-tracks, it would include three AMX tanks, the brigade reccy unit, one battery of 120 mm mortars and an air liaison team.

Gur decided to lead with his strongest rifle company, followed by the tanks, then the support company, the reccy unit and the air tentacle, with mortars at the tail. His ablest platoon leader, Lieut. Arieh Crespi, would ride as point in the first half-track. Gur, though in command, would go in the third half-track. The ground and the possibilities of ambush considered, it was not a promising arrangement since it directly risked isolation of two commanders.

But Gur was counting strongly that he could maintain control by radio even if surprised. It seemed simple enough as the force formed up on the desert pike. Though the last element was more than one mile to the rear, he found by test that he was in radio touch with every group leader.

At the last moment two additions were ordered which made the column more ponderous and control more complex. One battery of 25-pounders was added and the third rifle company, truck-mounted, was put ahead of the reccy unit.

At exactly 1230 hours Gur signaled for the move. From excitement, all hands must have gunned it, for within less than thirty minutes Crespi in the lead half-track was already entering the pass, and Gur in the third vehicle was three hundred yards behind his point, scarcely seeing him because of the dust cloud.

Here the desert road climbs sharply as it approaches the mountains, then dips abruptly where it starts running along the canyon floor. None in Gur's command had seen this road before. None was aware that the rise and fall and twisting of the right of way would automatically deprive the column of front-to-rear unity. Expecting a romp, none had anticipated the operational problem.

As Gur topped the rise, he heard shots. Crespi's voice came

over the radio: "They're shooting at me; not heavy yet."

Gur said, "Keep going! Keep going!" Such was his own momentum that he had no time to think this problem out. No premonitory warning came in the second which made the difference between an irrevocable commitment and a force still under control and responding to his wish.

Now his own half-track careened downgrade and bullets zinged overhead. Here both the road and the canyon widened perceptibly. The fire intensified. To the whine of bullets was added the bang of mortars. Still, the group with Gur rode unscathed. Again Gur yelled to Crespi, "Keep going!"

Crespi called back, "I can't. We're losing men. My steering wheel's knocked out. We're stuck."

Gur said, "I'm coming up to you and take you out." It was his intention now to rescue Crespi, and back the whole column out of the canyon. He had been ordered to do no hard fighting. But the decision came a few seconds too late. When hit, Crespi had already doubled the distance which separated him from his commander and was lost to sight around a bend in the canyon. For reasons which Gur could not then understand, the column was already fractionalized.

Momentarily Gur halted his own half-track. He radioed the AMX's: "Follow me and shoot up the canyon walls as we move." They rode hellbent toward Crespi. It was Gur's plan to ride on past Crespi's wrecked point vehicle and use the tanks as a base of fire to cover the rescue act. A sound enough procedure, but wholly unrelated to the circumstances.

As this small task force veered round the bend in the canyon, it passed the second half-track, now ditched. To stop and see what had happened to its people was impossible. The bend was a death trap, the center of fire from both canyon walls and from both directions. Automatic weapons, mortars, rockets and rifles all ranged in on it. All hands with Gur crouched low. But the beat of bullets on the thin hull was incessant and mortar shards bouncing from the rock cliffs beat a tattoo on floor and flesh.

Suddenly the road narrowed and became half blocked by a wrecked Egyptian truck. Gur's driver stopped. Figuring that any attempt to get out and deploy would be group suicide, Gur yelled, "Push it off! Keep going!" One well-aimed shunt, and the stalled truck toppled into the roadside ditch. The half-track raced on another two hundred yards.

There two things happened coincidentally: Gur's party broke free of the zone of intense fire, and the half-track was confronted by another stalled enemy vehicle blocking the road. The half-track tried, but this wreck couldn't be budged, and there was no detour around it.

Upslope not more than fifteen yards were several empty sangars (rifle pits) revetted with loose rock. They promised cover. Gur told his people, "Get up into those holes." He wanted a few moments to think out his situation. A few aimed rifle shots were now dusting the truck and the roadway. It seemed that in this pause the sangars would be safer.

With Gur went his driver, signal officer, three riflemen and Captain Voxey, commander of the lead company. They had climbed and settled into the sangars before Gur realized that his party was alone. Concerned with what happened forward, he had not looked backward. No half-track followed him. None but his own group could profit by his example.

So he bent to his radio, trying to make contact. He was still stooped low in the sangar at that futile task when around the canyon bend straight toward him raced some of the following half-tracks.

The loaded men were not crouched low. They were standing and firing upward, shouting like demons. Gur stood in the sangar, waved his arms and yelled, "Hold it! Hold it! Stop now!" So did the men around Gur.

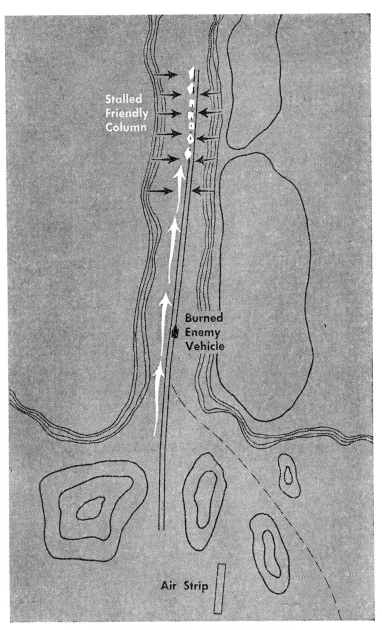

MOVEMENT INTO THE GAUNTLET

They could have spared their breath. That part of the serial whipped by, not a man hearing or seeing his commander fifteen yards away, such was the din and excitement of the situation. How the vehicles got past the obstacle which had blocked Gur stays unexplained. Maybe the lead track succeeded in shoving it aside; more probably, Gur had overestimated the difficulty.

Gur yelled to Captain Voxey in the next sangar, "Go down to the road and stop anyone else who comes along."

Voxey started.

Seconds later a rifleman from out of the same pit yelled to Gur, "Voxey's gone."

Gur yelled back, "Don't be nervous; I sent him."

The boy cried, "You don't understand; he's *gone*."

Gur said, "Yes, I know it."

The boy stood, trembling. Words no longer came. He simply pointed. Gur looked. Stretched not six feet below him was Voxey's body. He had taken a bullet through the head. The boy could not bear to say, "My captain's dead." This often happens to men in battle.

The sangar position was getting worse by the moment. Intense bullet fire was now beating against the rock walls from directly upslope, crossing automatic fire from the opposite canyon wall.

Since both cliffs rose almost straight from the road, the sangars, which rested on a narrow shelf near the base, afforded no cover. It was much like expecting the earth banks at the bottom of a well to serve as protection from missiles tossed over its rim. Each rock circle was a bull's-eye. Gur and the others survived only because Egyptian marksmanship was so poor.

Belatedly Gur noted a narrow gully which, from the road, cut into the cliff briefly several rods away. He pointed and yelled to his men, "Run for it!" They obeyed and he followed. It was an unorderly scamper.

On settling into the gully, his first thought was to raise other parts of the column by radio. Only then did he realize that his set was missing, and at first he couldn't remember what had happened to it.

The command AMX had come to rest seventy yards farther along the road and was machine-gunning the canyon walls. Gur sent one of his riflemen on the run to the tank commander, saying, "Tell him to go on through the pass, round up all my people and bring them back here." His idea was that if he could get enough men to form a line, he might find a path up the cliff and attack the Egyptian positions from the westward.

Worrying about the half-track which he had left helpless along the road, Gur at last remembered how he had lost the radio. Voxey had been carrying it when he was shot down. Another rifleman volunteered to return to the sangars and retrieve it. The set was still working.

Soon Gur was talking to Sergeant Eitan of Crespi's platoon. Then he learned for the first time that the two lead half-tracks had become ditched together, though, as he sped by, he had seen only one.

Eitan said, "Crespi's dead. We've had four others killed. There are about six wounded around me. My people are down between the half-tracks and the cliff wall. We can't move out of here and we can't stay."

He told why. Machine guns had zeroed in on both ends of his protection. Other weapons from the cliff opposite were centering fire on the rock wall just above his head. Bullets bouncing from the road and off the cliffside were causing all of his losses.

Eitan said, "Two half-tracks from the support company

have stopped just a few yards from me. I don't know why. Also, an ambulance has drawn into this block. Every minute we lose another man."

Wistfully Eitan concluded, "Can't you give me a little fire?"

Gur answered, "Yell to the commander of the support company. Get him on your radio."

Soon Lieutenant Rubicheck was at the set, saying to Gur, "I've got many men wounded, including the doctor, and several men killed. The doctor's in the ditch, pinned by fire. He says the wounded need plasma. It's in the ambulance. That spot's too hot for anyone to get through."

It was an overestimation. While Rubicheck talked, Sergeant Eitan darted from behind the tracks and ran for the ambulance. He jumped through the door and onto a pile of dead men. These bodies he stacked on the far side of the vehicle to give him protection while he hunted for the plasma. This insulation doubtless saved his life. Automatic fire beat against the side of the vehicle like a triphammer and was ripping it apart. Now well elevated above the road, Eitan could see why.

Hull down, in a dug-in position atop a knob which nestled next to the opposite cliff wall not more than thirty-five yards away, was a Russian-made half-track. On it were mounted the two machine guns which kept Rubicheck's people pinned. Such was the angle that the enemy position and its people remained hidden to the Israeli fighters in the roadside ditch.

Eitan got back with both the plasma and the information. On radio, Rubicheck gave Gur a fill-in.

"Try both bazooka fire and rifle grenades," said Gur. "One or the other will take out the half-track. Meanwhile, if one of the tanks gets back, I'll try to put artillery on it."

Briefly and bitterly, Gur reflected on the irony of his own

position in the gully. Having directed that the half-tracks
which had broken through the ambush should return and
assemble on him, for the moment his command post was in-
flexibly rooted to one spot amid a fluid fight. Should he move
to co-ordinate the attack on the roadblock to the eastward,
greater confusion might result.

There was one consoling afterthought: in such a frag-
mented situation, one starting point was likely to be as good
as another. When no clear choice was presented, the main
needs were firmness at one point and a little luck.

The decision to stick it was the turning point. Luck and
firmness arrived together. Where Rubicheck's men had hud-
dled beneath the killing fire, their wills benumbed by it, the
restored contact with Gur already was having a catalytic effect,
re-energizing the actors. It is ever thus with men whose spirits
wither because no one points the way out. Firm orders and a
redefinition of task are the springboard to moral recovery.

From the roadside ditch two rifle grenadiers opened fire on
the target described by Eitan. A bazooka team crawled down
the road a piece so as to get at the half-track from the blind
side of the knob.

Simultaneously the AMX messenger returned from his er-
rand of recalling the runaway platoons aboard the half-tracks.

"I stopped them," he said to Gur. "They were over a mile
down the road, pulled up and wondering what to do. Everything's quiet on that end. They're turning around. In five
minutes, they should be here."

While Danny, the signal officer, went to the telephone on
the hull of the AMX, Gur stayed at his radio. The idea in this
relay was that Rubicheck would observe fire, report to Gur,
who would pass the word to Danny, who would correct the
laying. But the target was masked by the bend in the road and
the data was hazy. Tanks are not built to knock out obscure

hilltop positions. Not one shell exploded where Rubicheck could see it.

The failure did not matter. Suddenly the enemy half-track started burning and next to it a cache of ammunition exploded. The best guess of those who saw the action is that the bazooka team made the kill.

When that word came over radio, the AMX elevated its gun and began to shell the caves along the cliff top. That was an extra precaution. In Gur's part of the canyon all enemy weapons had gone quiet when the half-track exploded.

Impatient, Gur sent the AMX on a second mission to hurry the half-tracked companies back to him. Seconds after the tank departed, Gur was buzzed by the commander of the reserve company which had entered the canyon on trucks. It was still whole, having come along slowly and not yet advanced into the fire zone.

Also, he heard on radio from the commander of the reccy unit. Its people had come into the fire zone and, though stalled not too far behind Gur, were "ready to fight" if given orders. So Gur told them to attack up the sides of the canyon and clean up the pockets of resistance which seemed to be lodged somewhere along the cliff structure near the top.

They tried to obey. At a distance, Gur saw them climb the slope hand over hand. Thrice they closed on the decisive ground and thrice they formed and charged. Each time they seemed to break just as they were at the point of success.

Gur, the eyewitness, was completely baffled. He thought it was his own fire from the canyon floor which was withering the charge; and, nursing this illusion, he called over the radio for his own riflemen and half-tracks to suspend action. Nothing good came of that order; it didn't help the reccy unit but it did cause the Egyptian fire to build higher against the men in the roadside ditches. Much later Gur learned that it was the shooting of Egyptian marksmen from the opposite canyon wall which had dissolved the reccy attack. Not being able to see or hear it above the confusion of sounds and sights much closer to him, he had misread the situation. For the moment, he was disappointed in his men rather than chagrined at his own error, and had he been able to see all things clearly, he would have felt much better.

Things were looking up. The column was still disjointed and strung out over three and one-half miles of road, half of which was a fire gauntlet. Gur had been given a bad seventy minutes. But he contented himself with the thought that in that brief time he had seen control dissolve and vanish and that the command was now coming back solidly to his hand.

That largely fortuitous outcome, however, left unresolved both his own tactical situation and decision at the brigade level about what further should be done. Due to heady optimism at both levels, the battalion, ordered to conduct only a reconnaissance in force, had blundered into a well-set trap and been stung. Its experience was almost identical with the entrapment of American columns by fire gauntlets rigged by the Red Chinese during the great battle of November, 1950, in North Korea. Once committed and split apart, the infantry and armor elements of these columns, one south of Kunuri, the other north of Kotori, had tried to fight their way through. Of this had come heavy loss and inexplicable local defeat.

The main lesson from those operations was that when a road column moves into a defile, and becomes ambushed from both flanks, its disorganization is likely to be rapid and continuous if its elements persist in the attempt to break through via the road.

Gur had called his people back mainly out of compliance with the spirit of the initial order. But he was still of mixed mind whether he could and should withdraw or, having become stuck, was still better placed than the rear of the brigade to destroy the Egyptian resistance along the cliff tops.

But the problem was Sharon's, not his. There was first the question of whether it was better to fight now and, if the answer was yes, what means and what plan should be chosen. Sharon could not be sure that Gur's battalion either retained sufficient hitting power or could reassemble for movement without once more drawing the lightning.

6...Hand to Hand

GUR'S small picture of the fight was almost a blank. He could see the rock walls, some of his wrecked vehicles and a few of his own men. But he could get no idea of the location of the enemy fire positions which were killing his strength.

From where Sharon sat, the problem was still more obscure. Hearing nothing from Gur, he could sense what had developed only from the distant noise. Having sent his deputy with the task force, he had no choice but to wait and worry. What hadn't been foreseen was that the canyon structure would blot out radio communication.

At 1430 came a written message from the deputy, Colonel Hossi, delivered by officer-runner. It said, "I'm stuck. I can't locate the enemy positions. I propose to attack up both sides of the pass. But to get started, I must have help."

The courier said, "He's fairly well back in the column. From where we were we could get no idea what was happening more than a few feet away from us." The courier told what he had observed but there wasn't much to go on.

Sharon immediately put his two batteries of 25-pounders into action shelling both sides of the pass. Two artillery observers had gone forward with the task force. He figured the FO's might see the bursts, get on radio and regulate the fire. It was a vain hope. The brief bombardment was a sheer waste of ammunition and was soon called off.

Then the Second Infantry Battalion, led by Lieut. Col. Aaron Davidi, was lorried forward. The artillery battalion commander rode with it to see if he could help with controlled fire. Gur by this time was getting the nucleus of his battalion in hand. Second Battalion closed to within one-half mile of the pass, then deployed and started climbing the right-hand cliff. They made it to the top but found nothing—except empty positions.

Forming a line, they moved forward several hundred yards along the cliff top. Then their eyes took in the problem. Looking at the opposite cliff, they could see many small caves in its face, almost closed by piled-up rock. These caves were so far down the cliff wall that from the angle on the height, it was impossible to put fire into them.

What they saw, including the wreckage of First Battalion's transport strewn for three miles along the road below, was flashed by radio to the brigade. Sharon at last had eyes for the battle. It was his first solid information.

Second Battalion guessed that both cliff walls had been recessed with fire caves such as they could see on the face opposite. So, not waiting for an order, the men started down the cliff to get at the holes nearest to them.

But the cliff had an almost sheer face. To negotiate it, the men had to hold on with both hands, slinging their rifles. So moving, they were easy marks for the concealed Egyptian riflemen on the other side of the canyon. Many were shot down; others tried to get going. It became an individual battle. Several of the enemy cave parties were mopped up. Later Egyptian and Israeli dead were found together in the holes.

Sharon had made the mistake of calling for an air strike against the cliff tops. It came in while this grapple was proceeding along the canyon wall. He had to wave it off lest it kill his own men and stampede Second Battalion.

MITLA PASS CLIFF STRUCTURE (Note: One side of the canyon is cut away in this illustration. D marks the beginning of the gauntlet. A brackets the area of the heaviest defensive fires and the Israeli counterattack.)

Not more than three or four minutes after the friendly jets turned back toward base (the hour was 1550) six MiG's and four Meteors pounced on the pass from the westward. They strafed the cliff edge on both sides of the canyon, raked the stalled column on the roadway and came straight on to the brigade camp to plaster it with rockets.

Quite fortuitously, it seemed to Sharon, two Israeli Ouragans came out of nowhere, took on the MiG's and sent them high-tailing toward Suez. But the Meteors turned for a second pass and strafed the camp again.

A little too late, Sharon saw the downhill attack as a blunder. Losses were mounting fast and he was getting nothing from it. As so often happens in a fire fight, he had been sucked in prematurely by the rhythm of engagement when main tactical advantage was on the other side, though time itself would work in his favor. The game had absorbed him more than the ground.

Still, there had been an unforeseen dividend from it. The down-cliff sorties had drawn the Egyptian fire upward and away from the people pinned to the rocks next to the roadway. In this hard-won respite, Sharon relayed word to Colonel Hossi to collect the task force. Letting the vehicles go, he would displace the men the minimum distance westward that would get them out of fire. Due to Gur's dogged collecting effort, it was more easily done than had been anticipated.

Abruptly, Sharon ordered Second Battalion to call off the cliffside scramble, get atop the scarp again and await instructions. His mind was just now forming the new plan. But to play the string out, he ordered his antitank guns into the pass experimentally, just on the chance that they might be able to silence the caves by direct fire. The angle made it a futile effort.

Observers along the cliff top told him about a burning enemy vehicle which lay seemingly beyond the area where the Egyptian fire gauntlet was still effective; it was the same Russian-built half-track which Gur had sent his bazooka team after.

That, Sharon decided, would mark the line for reassembly and subsequent counterattack. Still divided, the force was told to hold the pass even with this beacon.

Second Battalion advanced still farther westward along the cliff top. Individually, or in small groups, First Battalion flanked this advance as its men regrouped on the canyon floor. There was an hour or so for rest before dark fell.

At 1730 hours the fight was resumed. Two companies advanced from west to east along the cliff top. The other two companies attacked along the road and scrambled up the cliff face to the spider holes. That would box the enemy in; also, it was reasoned that it would be safer to climb up than down. If the treatment worked along one cliff, it was to be repeated on the other side.

Sharon's belated realization that the night attack favored his side was based on the simple proposition that after dark the Egyptian marksmen on the opposite cliff could not see to shoot.

The operation lasted two hours. It was hardly a fight. The dark made most of the difficulty. There was no close grappling, and in the nature of their positions, no possibility of a general Egyptian surrender. In night defense, unified resistance in any soldiery depends on seeing or feeling that collected fire is keeping the odds fairly even. The cellular manner of the Egyptian distribution forbade it, once the light faded. Each part was on its own and therefore useless.

One by one the cells collapsed with hardly a sputter as the mop-up proceeded from one cliff to the other. Hand grenades, bazookas, machine pistols and boulders were the weapons used. By 2000 hours all firing had ceased and Mitla Pass was solidly in the hands of the brigade.

During the mop-up Sharon learned from prisoners that he was dealing with the Fifth and Sixth Battalions of the Egyptian Second Brigade. Later 211 of their dead were buried in the earth of Mitla Pass.

Sharon's Brigade lost 34 killed and 102 wounded, which made this unintended engagement relatively the costliest fight in the Sinai war. It was by now a badly battered outfit, still heavily weighted with the task of carrying its casualties down from the heights for nighttime evacuation. The men kept at it.

Just before midnight, another message came through to Sharon that the Egyptian armored brigade based on Bir Gifgafa seemed to be moving toward him. They were close enough that he might be hit before dawn. So now the problem was to reorganize the brigade for defense in two directions; the other enemy brigade, based on Shalufa, was only one hour's ride distant. Still, since Sharon's brigade now outposted the pass, and its detachments on the heights could block the defile with relatively little fire, as the Egyptians had done, it was clear that the armored threat from the rear was the main danger.

By this time the Israeli brigade of tanks under Colonel Ben-Ari had extended its flank far enough south to partly counter such a threat. But since Sharon did not have this piece of information, for his purposes it might as well not have been there.

All of the wounded had been brought down from the cliffs and were under medical care by midnight. Refueling had been completed. Sharon called the commanders together to hear orders for reorganization. They came with dragging feet. Sharon started talking. Once again, the men facing him all fell asleep.

Though temporarily the brigade stayed sprawled, Sharon made no attempt to arouse the conference. The Army of Israel well understands that exhausted men cannot fight; its officers are taught that even a few minutes of sleep may turn a beaten fighter into a champion. Worse than the risk of being surprised is that of trying to engage when the physical power in one's own force is almost totally depleted.

These are simple guides to action. By most commanders today, they are honored more in the breach than in the observance. Israel's Army is an exception. Sharon lay down and slept beside his officers for four hours, telling the sergeant on duty when to awaken him. The others got up refreshed and he gave them their orders.

There had been no sign of the enemy. The Egyptian armor, feeling itself heavily embattled, though such was not the case, stayed glued to the central axis. The enemy brigade near Suez didn't stir.

At 0400 hours Sharon regrouped his force into four small

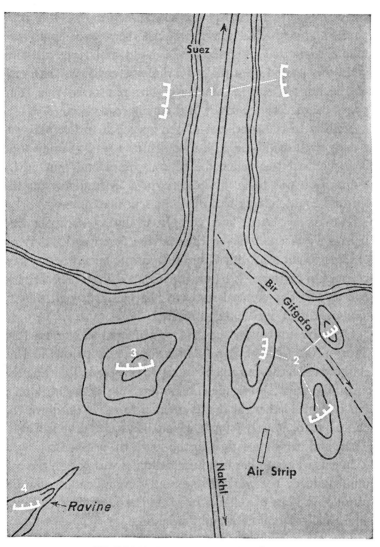

SHARON'S DEFENSIVE POSITIONS

teams. The one which manned the "front line" where the cliffside fight had taken place, was formed of two rifle companies and a few heavy weapons. Another two-company battalion, supported by three AMX tanks and three antitank guns, was posted on a rocky foothill somewhat to the north of the brigade rear. Team three—one reinforced rifle company—guarded to the south of the main road.

Slightly to the southeast of the approach to the pass was a deep slash in the earth, the branch of a wadi. Sharon used it to conceal two reduced rifle companies and four AMX tanks. This was to be his reserve, held in readiness for the surprise counterattack if the Egyptian armor came on.

The redeployment was completed during dark. At first light, a Piper was sent out to scout the desert and the Wadi el Hegayib almost to Bir Gifgafa. It saw no enemy armor anywhere. On getting this report, the camp relaxed. The brigade had its first day of total rest. On Sharon's order, all activity was suspended, including patrolling.

On 2 November the brigade was ordered to capture Ras-Sudr on the Gulf of Suez. Earlier, one of its patrols had reconnoitered a caravan track leading to this place. Quitting the main highway, the brigade entered Ras-Sudr at daybreak on 3 November. That night it was ordered to move on down the coastal road, join the force which had been dropped at E Tour, and carry on with it to the south tip of Sinai.

In this way, another two hundred miles was put on the column's already overworked transport, doubly loaded now because of the loss of vehicles in Mitla Pass. But it was all vain endeavor, waste motion and no fighting.

The last maneuver had been ordered "just in case." Twenty miles short of Sharm-El-Sheikh and Tiran Island, the brigade was stopped by High Command and told to head for home base, four hundred miles distant. Its side of the pincers wasn't needed. The tip of Sinai and control over the water passage next to it had already been won by another brigade fitted with seven-league boots.

For Sharon's men, the campaign ended in disappointment. The general feeling of the brigade was chagrin that its effort had been something of a side show, contributing only indirectly to decision.

7...West to Suez

O N loosing his small field army into Sinai, Maj. Gen.
Moshe Dayan was faced with a main problem not soluble in sensible terms.

The great obstacle to a clean sweep of the peninsula lay directly northwest of Queisima athwart the central desert highway running to Ismailia in the Canal zone.

Though this was the nightmare, it was not so because Abu Agueila was made more formidable than all else through a preponderant concentration there of enemy fighting forces.

In numbers of men and count of guns, Egypt's greater strength was deployed in and around the defensive complex at the coastal village of Rahfa, which covered the back entry into the Gaza Strip and guarded the front door to El Arish, the main base of supply for Egyptian forces east of Suez.

If the Rahfa fortifications could be dealt one smashing blow by an attack staged across flat ground, approaching by night and using relatively conventional tactics, the whole enemy flank in the north might fall apart.

That this was clearly envisaged by Israel's General Staff prior to mobilization is reflected in the plan. The attack against Rahfa was made a set piece. The participating brigades got firm assignments early and, with slight change in theme and variation, carried through to the finish.

What developed around Abu Agueila on the central axis was in absolute contrast. There was no orthodox, proved way to get hold of it, due to the deficiencies in Israel Army's support establishment, and not less to the High Command's resolve to keep losses minimal.

The Abu Agueila position was a hedgehog of three successive, strongly fortified sand ridges which crossed the main road at right angles to it. The distance between the front and rear of this considerable obstacle was about six miles, when the rear-guard post in Abu Agueila village is considered.

All three ridges were fixed with deep, solidly walled trenches and bunkers according to the best German design. All were armed with spliced-in field artillery and tank-killing guns. Some armor was known to be within the hedgehog, and approximately one Egyptian brigade of infantry was distributed over its works. Each position was beautifully protected by concertinas and an encircling barrier of double-apron barbed wire. In fact, such barriers were multiple, and each enclosed an antitank mine field.

Eastward of the foremost and largest sand ridge, the approach ground was perfectly flat for several miles.

Neither this ridge nor the two behind it could be outflanked from the north because of an impassable natural obstacle.

To the southward, the prospect was hardly better. No road lay that way, and no thoroughfare, due to the frequent straight-sided basaltic peaks which erupted into the otherwise fairly flat desert landscape.

On that flank, beyond the desert, was a mountain range, the Jebel Dalfa, barren and sharp-toothed. It is split by a defile called the Dyka Pass, through which an Egyptian road runs from Bir Hasne to the main road near Abu Agueila. By detouring on a roundabout westerly course and coming up and over this pass, the attackers might strike at the hedgehog from its rear. A branch road led to the south lip of the nearest fortified ridge, Umm Gataf.

But this was an adventure to give nightmares to any nor-

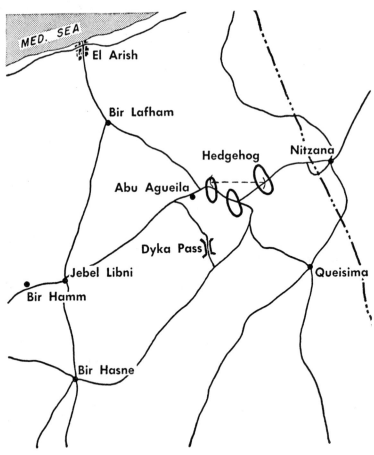

THE ABU AGUEILA HEDGEHOG

mally minded tanker, if such there be. Moreover, if the Shermans and AMX's got through at all—which must have been regarded as doubtful—their passage would chew up the one crude trail so badly as to make all but impossible the task of supplying them by truck convoy.

So doing, they might be committed to enemy country, short-handed, with no good chance of backing away. On the other hand, to maintain them through air-dropped bundles was altogether out of the question since Sharon's Brigade was monopolizing Israel's air-borne lift capacity.

This was the obstacle. Left unanswered, while other plans went forward, was the main question of whether to hit it with a hammer or toy with it experimentally.

By the first alternative, the High Command would have decided at the outset to attack Umm Gataf frontally in decisive strength—perhaps three brigades—and reconcile itself to the attendant losses.

By the second choice, it would poke at the hedgehog by exploring the difficult approaches from the southward and exploiting such opportunities as were found.

In the end, it followed neither course resolutely and exclusively. What it tried was a compromise: there was mounted a half-armed attack via the direct approach, while, almost empirically, the probing effort from the south flank was put in motion, with ultimate consequences which exceeded all expectation.

It is the one touch of equivocation, of doubt, and possibly of unnecessary waste in the management of the general battle by Israel's High Command. Its General Staff is still divided about whether that which eventuated was the best possible solution, some members raising the question whether it would not have been better to go straight in and swing for a knockout.

While the argument is not likely to be resolved by those who, seeing the prize more clearly than the forfeits, study the campaign from a distance, what happened in the event supplies at least one point in rebuttal. Nothing was wasted via the indirect approach. There, at least, opportunity was made to pay overtime. More troops could not have been put forward and supplied over the primitive and geographically treacherous lines of communication which had to be used. Those who got to the battle proved prodigious almost beyond understanding.

In the beginning, one reserve infantry body, Brigade C, none too well prepared, badly rushed and filled with more eagerness than information and caution, was sent frontally against Umm Gataf, the foremost and strongest ridge. It was kicked back on its heels, having lost a few men while gaining wisdom. The attack proved only that this was the wrong way to reduce Umm Gataf. The Egyptians were not quitting. After its first futile pass, the brigade was saved to fight another day. Its frustration but raised the question what should next be done.

The inadequacy of this preliminary probe toward Umm Gataf, plus the fact that Colonel Ben-Ari's brigade of armor had been ordered to Queisima with its task still not set, though four possible missions had been described to it tentatively, shows that what to do about Abu Agueila remained the one unanswered question up till the hour when the battle began to develop.

But to describe it also as the only point of indecision in the High Command management of operations would be wrong as either praise or criticism. Whereas the aim from the beginning was all-inclusive and Israel intended nothing less than the uprooting of all Egyptian force in Sinai in the shortest possible time, what could be preplanned in tactical operations, and preset through the assignment of appropriate forces, was determined by the grip of supply and of transport facilities. Firm plans, to be realistic, must stem from sufficiency of hitting forces and material resources. When they cannot be stretched far enough to cover the battle from first to last, determining what is best left to the battle's chance and the knock of opportunity is in itself one form of decision.

Thus when total invasion was launched, the question mark stayed suspended above the fortified ridges at Abu Agueila, and what final employment would be given Ben-Ari and his brigade, already staged into enemy country at Queisima, remained vague.

Here was one of the most solid hitting bodies in the Israeli Army, still held on leash within a few hours' ride of the most formidable enemy target in Sinai.

It was a "regular" brigade in the sense that most of its units were filled with inductees then doing their active training; that is how the word is used in Israel when applied to units other than reserves. There are no enlisted volunteers. However, many of the attachments of the brigade, such as pioneer platoons, maintenance groups and signal units, were formed wholly of reservists, who had to be received, equipped and folded into their operating positions before this "regular" brigade could move.

Its fighting power was embodied mainly in one battalion of Sherman medium tanks, one battalion of light AMX tanks, one battalion of motorized infantry and a scout or reconnaissance company which moved on half-tracks. Rather than keep these battalions separate during combat, Ben-Ari liked to scramble his forces, hitting with three balanced teams.

Perhaps better primed for the war than any other combat element in the Army, the battalion of medium tanks, with its complement of armored infantry, had been on field exercises in the Beersheba area during the preceding thirty days, concentrating on movement procedures in company- and platoon-size operations.

Commanding the battalion was pint-sized Lieut. Col. Avra-ham Adan, aged 39. No one in Israel's Army ever calls him other than "Bren," which nickname derived not from any personal predilection for that British-made weapon, but as a contraction of "Avraham." Square-set, blond-headed, shy of manner but with a bubbling sense of humor, Bren is a fighter worth watching. He was born in Palestine and poverty. Of public schooling and formal military education, he had what he got as a member of the Palmach, the underground striking force in the War of Independence. Warm-natured as are most sabras, Bren is a soldier's soldier. Close acquaintance with him merely ripens the first impression that he was born to lead well in battle but would not shine in any other environment.

That, at least, he had in common with his brigade com-mander, Ben-Ari, though probably not much more. Ben-Ari was born in Prussia and migrated to Palestine as a youth. Yet, paradoxically, he has all the personal mannerisms of a Junker among German generals—almost unbending formality, curt speech, a certain grimness, brusque gesturing, impatience with the conversation of others and a tendency to oversimplify all that nature made complex. His face, figure and carriage fit that same part. In his command manner and surface person-ality characteristics, he is so unlike other Israeli military lead-ers, and bears such striking resemblance to the Prussian mili-tary type, that any social scientist might be interested in studying how he got that way.

Ben-Ari's brigade gathered at an assembly area just a few miles south of Nitzana (El Auja) during Sunday, 28 October. There the reservists formed on the "regulars." Bren's bat-talion did the forty-three miles from Beersheba in daylight, riding on its own tracks, since no tank transporters were available.

Dismal is the word for this concentration. The brigade had no tank trucks for the hauling of fuel. The assembly area was twelve miles from the nearest highway. There was no flat, traversable ground across which to array its strength. All of the readying-up services had to be performed with the vehicles far strung out in column along one inadequate trail.

Even so, the brigade's difficulties were but a minor note in a large picture of confusion. Temporarily the whole Army was half convulsed by its first experience with a showdown national mobilization.

One prime mistake had been made. The people had been called up. But civilian transportation had been mobilized at the same time. It hadn't been foreseen by the General Staff that these things don't go together, if movement is to be maintained. When the reservist was called to report to his depot and form with his unit under arms, if he happened to be a trucker or a bus driver, that simply stalled the vehicle which the Army also needed.

So for two days there was semistagnation and high crisis. When it became evident that the plan was breaking down, the Army moved detachments onto the main highways and set up roadblocks. Trucks and buses were commandeered as they came along and sent where troops and supply were waiting to be hauled. One lesson of the campaign was that Army organic transportation had to be increased. The emergency measures stripped some of the villages of both their food and the means to haul it.

Ben-Ari had been told that his brigade should be ready to move at dawn on D-Day plus one, which meant Tuesday, 30 October. He didn't know where and for the time being that was his smallest concern. The brigade was out of fuel; the gasoline didn't arrive until late the last night. Thereupon the battalions were told to cut their ammunition supply by two thirds and use the extra space to carry additional gas and oil. Each tank carried eighty artillery rounds and one hundred gallons of fuel. Its reserve was cut to twenty rounds to accommodate the fuel load.

Earlier on that day, Ben-Ari had called Bren to his CP, handed him some pretty new map sheets of North Sinai, and said, "Get familiar with these." Bren took them away but didn't look again. He still awaited his task and he saw no point in poring over maps until he knew where he was going to fight.

At sunset, both men got the word, in fact, several words. The brigade received orders to hit the road at dawn and head for Queisima, in case Harpaz needed help. Ben-Ari assembled his officers and said, "Part of Sharon's Brigade is right now in mid-air jumping into Sinai. We're in war." No pep talk followed. Nor did Ben-Ari voice his hunch that the brigade was probably bound for the Canal via the Ismailia road.

From the new situation, the first consequence to Bren was that, on order of High Command, one of his Sherman companies was detached to help the reserve brigade that was already maneuvering toward Umm Gataf. Next, his company of armored infantry was detached to move ahead of the brigade full speed toward Queisima. In this way, what had been a composite battalion (now called Task Force B) started its advance into Egypt as a single medium-tank company.

Bren knew that grief would come of this. During war, High Command may snatch units away at will; it's the way the game is played. But unless thereafter the commander lower down begs, bullies and bargains for their return, they are apt to stay gone too long, if not become forgotten. No other operational aberration makes for greater all-round unhappiness.

Bren was ready with the needle. When at 0600 hours he drew up to the Egyptian frontier, recognizing it from the line of stone markers along the ridge crest, he radioed Ben-Ari: "I'm moving into enemy country and I have no strength." Ben-Ari said, "Get going anyway." The entry was made for the sake of the record. Temporarily, the situation was safe enough. A reconnaissance patrol, under control of the brigade, had preceded Bren along the highway and had signaled to him: "Everything looks empty." It was typical of an army which during battle invariably puts all information in the vernacular.

By noontime, most of the brigade had made camp around Queisima, there to await the results of the reconnaissance in force toward Abu Agueila. Bren's unit sought natural cover, spread its camouflage nets and refueled the tanks. One Sherman had already lost a track to a mine alongside the road. Another had to be sent into Queisima to blast the houses down; a few Egyptian snipers had continued to operate from their cover. Otherwise the wait was without incident.

Ben-Ari was already long gone. In midmorning, the order came through that he should advance one battalion team only and "make contact with the enemy somewhere between Queisima and Abu Agueila." Except for the limitation on force, that let him write his own ticket. Choosing Task Force A for the mission, he decided to go along with the column.

Then he added one string to his bow. The reccy company would also advance on a related, but operationally detached, mission. While Task Force A moved over one north-running trail through the mountains, trying to get on the flank of Umm Gataf to test its strength, the reccy would swing out farther west and test the defenses of the Dyka Pass. If the probe indicated that the pass might be taken, the whole brigade might break through along that route and thereby get on the rear of the hedgehog at Abu Agueila.

So they started together under the high sun and within less than one hour the reccy column had moved beyond radio contact with Ben-Ari; through the afternoon, he had no idea how it was faring.

The commander spent these hours with the point of Task Force A lying just eight hundred yards off the south end of fortified Umm Gataf.

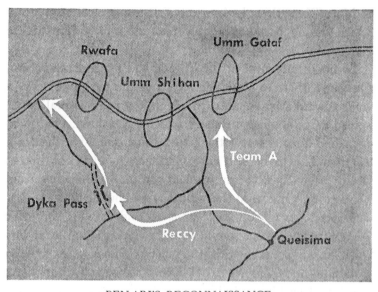

BEN-ARI'S RECONNAISSANCE

Ben-Ari didn't need to use his field glasses to see that Umm Gataf was formidably strong-ribbed and not to be taken for the reaching. Immediately upon descending to the low ground, his force had come under the fire of a battery of 25-pounders and a dozen or so "archers" shooting from the same line where the infantry was entrenched. One of his Shermans was robbed of its track by a fluke hit. The enemy artillery was wild, and the antitank guns especially were aiming way high. Feeling not too uncomfortable, he stayed there two hours or more trying to measure the position.

At the end he concluded that Task Force A alone was too weak to attempt storming the position. So he radioed higher headquarters, asking permission to bring the whole brigade up. The answer was this: "You can do it, provided that you don't get your armor mauled."

Ben-Ari felt that this pretty much tied his hands as to a direct assault on Umm Gataf. The fields of fire east, south and west of Umm Gataf were quite flat, with not a ravine or sand pimple to shield the approach along any line. To cross this ground without losing quite a few tanks would be impossible.

So decision on how best to employ the brigade would have to await hearing what had been learned by the reccy company. With that conclusion, he withdrew his force one mile, which got the Shermans beyond range of Umm Gataf's antitank guns though the Shermans could still put shellfire on the enemy ridge.

Still standing there, at 1600 hours Ben-Ari at last got word from his lost reccy company. To his astonishment, it was now directly west of him, just one mile off the main road leading to Ismailia, a league west of Abu Agueila village. That meant that instead of taking a look at the obstacle, the reccy had broken through Dyka Pass and gone on. It was now behind the farthest fortified ridge, alone, deep in enemy country. Ben-Ari said, "Stay there."

There is rhyme but no reason in what had happened. Dyka is a position almost identical with Mitla, a cliff-walled notch about two miles long threading the Jebel Dalfa barrier. Its sandstone walls run about five hundred feet high on both sides above the path, and the air space between the two walls of the canyon averages perhaps two hundred feet in width. The Egyptians had cut into these cliffs enough fire caves to seat a battalion. Along the base of each cliff was an elaborate arrangement of barbed-wire fences and mine fields. The roadway itself had also been systematically mined for demolitions.

Just short of Dyka Pass, on the approach from the south, is another fortified notch in the hills called The Straits. It also had been mined and pocked with fire caves. Had it been suitably manned, this double-barreled defile could not even have been challenged by Ben-Ari's armor.

But in their inscrutable way, the Egyptians had detailed but one platoon of sappers to hold both The Straits and Dyka Pass. When the reccy company nosed into the first of these, the few Egyptians scampered away without firing a shot. In flight, they stopped long enough to blow a bridge midway along the road to Dyka; that one good job forced the reccy company to stop and build a detour and some hours later badly slowed the passage of the brigade during the night. Also, a few craters were blown in the roadway, but the charges were too small to serve the purpose, and nothing much came of that except that, when the brigade banged through, one of Bren's Shermans, trying to avoid a crater, slipped off the edge into a ravine and was lost.

On getting the report from the reccy, Ben-Ari asked High Command on radio for permission to move the brigade via the Dyka Pass onto the rear of the enemy position at Abu Agueila. As dark fell, the approval came through.

But Ben-Ari left Task Force A in place, preparing for night defense directly south of Umm Gataf. Then in his command vehicle, he backtracked to Queisima to ready the main body. En route, he thought out his plan.

It was 1900 hours when he arrived at base and assembled his commanders for their orders conference. Everyone was weary. Facing them, Ben-Ari fell asleep before he could start talking. Thereby the conference was automatically suspended.

All present lay down and went to sleep for forty-five minutes.

On awakening, they got their tasks.

Task Force C would ride at once for Bir Hasne and capture it, thereby to afford some measure of protection to Sharon's Brigade from the enemy armor.

Force A, already at Umm Gataf, would stand ready to follow behind Force B after it had moved through the Dyka Pass.

Force B would be prepared to capture Abu Agueila village as soon as possible after dawn, following which, it would attack Rwafa, the rearward of the three ridges.

That didn't sound quite right to Bren, who at Queisima still had in hand just one company of Shermans. He said to Ben-Ari, "I'm too light to move; when will my other tanks be returned?"

Ben-Ari couldn't believe what he heard. He said, "I thought you had them. That detachment was canceled by High Command some hours ago." So it had been. But none of those to whom it really mattered had gotten the word.

However, getting the missing armor back quite clearly was to be Bren's job. Ben-Ari said to him, "You move the rest of your force out now, anyway." For an armored infantry company, Bren could pick up as a substitute the one that was now bivouacked with Force A somewhere along the road to Dyka.

So Bren sent his maintenance officer forth by jeep to scout the Army front and bring back the missing Sherman company.

It was easier said than done. By the time the officer found the company, it was deployed and attacking an outpost between Nitzana and Umm Gataf.

Tanks can't quit a fight just because a faraway boss is on the anxious seat. Another four hours passed before they disengaged and heard the message. By the time the messenger began piloting the Shermans along the road back, Bren's battalion, having picked up the armored infantry from Force A, was already so far into the mountains that it could not possibly be overtaken in time for the first fire fight.

That weakness in the van perforce required some slight modification of the attack plan during the ten-hour-long lurch of the brigade through the night and the Dyka. The march had started within one-quarter hour of the end of the conference. Its terrible difficulties need not be here described. Ben-Ari talked to Bren as they rode through the pass together.

Force B, with Bren leading, would capture Abu Agueila village soon after first light.

Force A would then leapfrog it and attack the fortified ridge extending from Rwafa dam.

That task finished, and Bren's lost Shermans having arrived, Force B would then pass through and assault Umm Shihan ridge.

That was how both men thought things would work out as the night waned and the column rolled out of Dyka and began the descent to the desert. Due to the wrecked bridge and the slow crawl of the armor around the detour, the march had killed two extra precious hours. In the end, that made quite a difference.

Ahead of the brigade, the reccy company waited. Normally, it rode in light tanks and jeeps. But its AMX's had been taken away to strengthen the battalions. It had made the Dyka Pass run in jeeps and weapons carriers. Its lone bivouac behind the Egyptian hedgehog had been maintained with machine guns and small arms.

8...Man in the Middle

JUST as dawn broke, Bren's battalion got to the Ismailia road and at the junction ran into the brigade reccy company which had blocked to the west of Abu Agueila throughout the night.

Some of its patrols had scouted toward Umm Shihan. Its commander, Maj. Izhak Ben-Ari, said, "The enemy unloaded three or four lorries of troops at the other crossroad. I think the highway to El Arish has been mined."

For safety's sake, Bren pared off one infantry platoon to guard the junction on his rear where Major Ben-Ari stood. There was no telling at what moment Colonel Ben-Ari might order the reccy company to go elsewhere.

Bren called his lead tank commander to say, "Get ready for a fight and keep moving." The tanks ran on. Two minutes passed. Then at one thousand yards' range the front tanks saw an Egyptian patrol in jeeps entering the intersection ahead. They fired. The Egyptians fled afoot, leaving the six jeeps, which were later captured.

Come within easy range of Abu Agueila village, the tank company deployed in line astride the road—and firing. Its zeal was excessive. Amid the huts, the enemy had an entrenched square, with a large pyramidal tent at its center. It was too conspicuous to be missed and too gossamery to be knocked down.

Bren's armor wasted forty rounds, riddling the tent but not shredding the canvas. Livid, he watched helplessly, yelling into his radio, "Stop it! Stop it! You're wasting ammunition." At long last his gunners got the idea. Maj. Moshe Brill later explained, somewhat feebly, that the gunners had been aiming for the trenches and missing.

Now shellfire descended on the column. It was 25-pounder fire coming from an eight-gun battery near the Rwafa dam, and it hit right along the road. Bren thought to himself, "Here I am moving into battle, already under shelling, and I have formed no plan." Much earlier, he had promised himself that in the predawn pause, after the battalion got through Dyka Pass and could assemble on the desert plain, he'd get his officers together and work something out.

But the night had been too short; there had occurred no pause and he had slipped up. Too late to repair the mistake, it was still time to use that familiar crutch which ever serves tardy control—fragmentary orders. On radio, he yelled, "Keep moving." Then he said, "Move faster!" And again, "Go all out!"

At the intersection ahead, he could see scores of Egyptian vehicles crowding the turn to flee toward El Arish. In the 1948 war, he had lost an action by failing to clear this same road at the same place.

It flashed in his memory, even as this new spectacle buoyed his confidence. The Egyptians were running; he'd take their whole hedgehog without blowing hard. His hope soared higher as radio brought news from the platoon dropped off to cover the crossroads on his rear: "We've just captured a convoy coming from the west; we have forty-three prisoners." Yes, it was going to be easy, if he could right now apply the pressure.

He said to Brill, "Take your tanks cross-country and capture the El Arish intersection." Making that detour, he would skirt the fire from the village.

Brill said, "It can't be done. North of the village the El Arish wadi wall is sheer rock, a hundred feet high."

Now the lead tanks were within two hundred yards of the closest house, and the shellfire from the Rwafa dam position grew incessant. Bren, from his position with the first infantry half-track, riding far forward as a point, could look into and beyond the village. What he saw gave him his first shock of the day.

Scuttling from house to house, or moving in the fire trench, he counted twelve enemy soldiers carrying rocket launchers. Their rounds were already bursting amid his armor. One pierced the second Sherman, knocking it out. Farther to the right, running down the wadi toward the village from the direction of Rwafa dam, came an Egyptian infantry company. Instead of fleeing, the enemy was counterattacking.

At that moment, the Egyptian artillery stopped action; Bren guessed it was because the opposing forces were at the point of becoming intermingled.

Bren said to the platoon leader in the first half-track, "Take your men, circle toward the bend in the wadi, attack that company in rear and destroy it." The man started a reply: "I don't think" and was permitted to get no further. Bren turned to his S-3 (operations officer), Lieutenant Abramovitch, saying, "Take this man's platoon and carry out the task."

Abramovitch did: he killed twelve Egyptians, captured a few and drove off the others. Simultaneously, the rest of Bren's armored infantry—two platoons—charged straight in and captured Abu Agueila village, losing four men wounded and another Sherman tank, knocked out by a rocket. The loot included two antitank guns, two armored personnel carriers, nineteen trucks and twenty-three prisoners. The skirmish was over by 0700 hours.

When he tried to call a commanders' conference amid the spoils, the Egyptian artillery again came down so hard and accurately that Bren said, "Mount up. We must quit the village."

They drove for the El Arish intersection, Bren still hesitating about his next step. As they made the crossroads, he at last saw clearly what he should do. The answer lay in the terrain.

In the corner northeast of where the roads met was a natural defensive position, just snug enough to hold his battalion, if it squeezed tight. Here the great dunes which flanked the road, running north as far as the eye could see, had not quite completed their conquest. Their edge pressed to within 130 yards of the intersection, thereby providing immunity to attack from the north, unless the enemy came via the road. Directly beside the roads west and south were four sharp-crested sand hills so that dunes and hills together formed a natural pocket. This higher ground on either side would afford the force some defilade, particularly from flat-trajectory weapons. If threatened with direct attack, the Shermans could nose out through the sand hills and fire down both roads.

It was the best cover, and the safest way to block the intersection. Since defensive time-marking was necessary, while awaiting the second company of Shermans, the position filled the bill.

To cover the two sides, Bren divided his force into two teams, one formed of an infantry company and a platoon of Shermans, the other counting one rifle platoon and two platoons of tanks. He told his men to spread out as much as possible to lessen the damage from the Egyptian artillery, and it struck him as odd that until dealing with the problem at hand, he had always believed that staying tight was the key to successful defense.

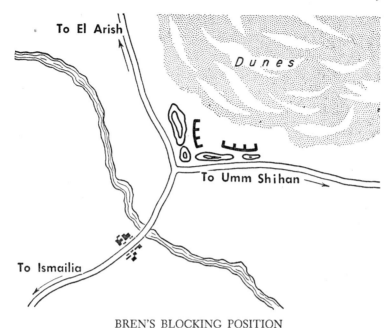

BREN'S BLOCKING POSITION

Came then two pieces of bad news. On radio, he was told that Task Force A, which was supposed to follow him into Abu Agueila, wouldn't be coming. Scenting large possibilities, Colonel Ben-Ari had figured out another mission for it, much farther to the west.

Coincidentally, Bren was told that his long-lost company of Shermans had almost caught up and was even then arriving at the road junction north of Dyka where he had been at dawn. But there was a postscript: because of the ploy which Ben-Ari was making with Task Force A to the westward, he would hold Bren's third company as his own reserve at the crossroads where they stood.

In war, Egyptians are a strange people. They so acted that morning, continuing to behave as if ignorant that the Israeli battalion was ambushing their highway pivot. Out of the east, they continued riding straight into the trap, with never an eye for the wreckage strewn about. In the first hour, the battalion knocked off forty-one enemy vehicles. But others kept coming, though the crossroads began to look like an automotive cemetery.

Then to the north Bren saw a great dust cloud rising. It was a body of Egyptian armor coming from El Arish: he knew that well enough before he saw the fifteen T-34's come in sight and take position two thousand yards off his flank.

While the enemy tanks deployed in line, another dust cloud rose in the east. Bren thought it was a second force of tanks coming from Umm Shihan. At two thousand yards, they still looked like armor, but they came on a little way more, and when they lined up, Bren could distinguish ten tank destroyers and several weapons carriers.

By now, the fifteen tanks to the north were firing. Bren's force ignored the shelling, centered its counterfire against the deployment to the eastward and knocked out one destroyer and three carriers. The others back-pedaled a little, and Bren's people suspended fire.

He didn't see it as a box. His ground remained well within range of both enemy groups. Together, they might have enough metal to crush him if they came on fast and took their losses. But he had fourteen good tanks and a superior defensive position; the margin satisfied him.

What frustrated him wholly was that in this situation he couldn't get hold of his other company of Shermans; he wanted to maneuver, get on the rear of the T-34's and drive them south. The terrain was "made to order" for it. So Bren prayed to Ben-Ari on radio and Ben-Ari "listened just a little." He promised to send Bren, well, maybe four of his tanks.

The T-34's fired for another twenty-five minutes; Bren didn't answer, having no shells to spare. Then the enemy tanks pulled back out of sight, returned a few minutes later, fired again, withdrew, returned, fired, and so on and on. Bren's people, charmed by this phenomenon, called it the "Egyptian Radio Waltz." There was no military explanation of what the enemy was doing. So they imagined that he was going through the motions to make more vivid a play-by-play description of a classic armored battle fraught with great fire and maneuver. Finding that idea amusing, the battalion felt less frustrated that its own guns could not return fire.

There were no identification panels in Bren's position; he had brought none when the battalion moved up. At noon, several Israeli jets came over the horizon, swept low and strafed the battalion with machine guns. Three men were wounded, one an outstanding platoon leader. There was a simple explanation of the blunder; information had lagged and the Israeli air thought Bren's people were still holding Abu Agueila village.

Through the afternoon, the position was shelled continuously by the tanks on the El Arish road, the destroyers deployed near Umm Shihan and the batteries based on Rwafa dam. It stayed inert under this double crossfire, not merely to conserve its short store of ammunition, but because any movement out from the protecting embankments would put the Shermans in a gut of flying steel.

What saved the force mainly was that the Egyptians used only armor-piercing rounds instead of high explosive. Either a hit was dead on, or it did little damage. Still, the aid station began to fill with wounded.

Ben-Ari called on radio saying, "I'm about to send your other tank company back; then you'll have to attack the reservoir position." Forthwith, Bren got in a jeep and, with Abramovitch, rode out to scout the ground forward where he would mount the attack. The reconnaissance took him within thirteen hundred yards of Rwafa dam, by which time he felt he had seen enough.

Then arose in his mind the question, "How should I employ my people?" The new tank company would arrive fresh and should therefore have more energy for the attack. On the other hand, the platoons which had borne the brunt through the day had also been looking at the critical ground all day and were therefore less likely to lose direction.

He decided—right or wrong—to use the fresh company to hold the defensive base and assault with the people already around him. There was another argument for it; the new company was still on the road, and if the assault plan was to become set in time, he'd have to deal at once with the officers who would lead it.

This was his spur-of-the-moment scheme of maneuver:

Directly across the road to his south was a fairly high, broad-surfaced sand hill, two thousand yards short of Rwafa dam. He would deploy two Sherman platoons there and they would provide covering fire for the assault force.

Two other platoons of Shermans would strike east, knock out the Egyptian strong point between him and Umm Shihan, then move southeastward in an arc so as to come up on the rear of the enemy batteries at the reservoir position.

This done, his armored infantry would move out via the road, and then veer southward so as to roll up the fortified ridge line from the flank. He figured the Shermans, by making the rear entry, would cool the position.

While riding back from the reconnaissance, he radioed his commanders to meet him at the CP. Several were there waiting, including one officer he had overlooked all day. The enemy shellfire had become thicker than ever.

The uninvited guest said, "I'm here for use; why haven't you been calling on me?" Bren flushed like a schoolboy. It was his forward artillery observer speaking, and all through that day Bren had clean forgotten that there were friendly guns at his disposal. Against himself, he chalked up another blunder.

Lying off to the south of the Umm Shihan position, near where the lorried infantry battalion was maintaining its clamp, was one battery of 25-pounders committed to the support of Ben-Ari's brigade. Bren's battle ground was just barely within range of these guns.

Bren said, "Go ahead. Bring in the fire. Put it against the armor on the El Arish road." It was done and the first salvo hit fair among the Egyptian tanks. They ceased fire and pulled back somewhat.

Bren gave his orders and the others moved out. The lift from their own artillery made it possible for the two companies to get into the assault position without becoming enfiladed. For some reason, the guns at the dam went silent when the T-34's ceased fire. It was the first blessed silence of the day. In this interval, the platoons made their sortie from the defensive pocket and on the open ground got set to spring, without a shot being fired. Lethargy had been heavy on Bren throughout the afternoon. Because of the stopping of the enemy fire, he felt quite suddenly refreshed. So it is with fighters when the fire pressure lifts. As danger seemingly recedes, the heart leaps up and unexpected energy floods back.

Amid calm, the quite orderly exit of his three assault elements gave Bren a buoyant confidence that the attack would go as planned. The fresh company had arrived in time and was already deployed around the defensive pocket.

The final touch was to notify Brigade by radio that the attack was on and the men were going forward.

Bren was in a hurry. Only a few minutes remained until sunset. If he timed his move exactly right, the last rays of day

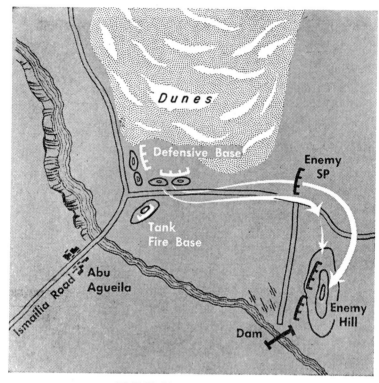

BREN'S PLAN OF ATTACK

would shine directly in the eyes of the Egyptians at the reservoir position as his men closed in. He told his forward observer to put artillery fire on that ground when he saw Bren's assault force spring from the line of departure.

Two platoons of Shermans advanced to the sand hill in the foreground to deploy along its crest and start the covering fire. The other two platoons of tanks drove east along the road going straight toward the Egyptian strong point that covered the intersection where the side road led to the dam.

Immediately, the shelling from the guns at the reservoir position resumed with doubled intensity. Enough artillery power was based there to make the night thunderous. Later the count of captured weapons at this one spot showed eight 25-pounders, eight 17-pounders mounted on tank destroyers, twelve 57 mm Czech-made antitank guns and two Boffers 40's. Now their crisscrossing fires threw a canopy of crimson flame over the battlefield which descended where Bren's men were moving to attack. To his eyes this spectacle wrought by the tracer rounds was at first more startling, more paralyzing, than anything he could see of the effect of the shellbursts on his men, now moving in the open.

Lighting the night, it warned him that he had gravely miscalculated the day. Moments before he had seen the red sun full and round just above the horizon. It had dropped like a plummet below the desert rim. The field was everywhere dark. His maneuver was barely begun; the objective was still two thousand yards distant.

When, on order, Bren's support artillery battery switched fire from the fourteen Egyptian tanks on the El Arish road to the fortified hill next to the reservoir, that again freed the enemy armor to fire into the backs of Bren's armored infantry. One half-track was hit dead on. But the opportunity was short-lived. The two platoons of Israeli tanks at the defensive base nestled among the sand hills at the corner of the dunes were there for the using. All day long tank ammunition had been husbanded toward this clutch, only seventeen rounds being fired to keep the Egyptians at distance. The Shermans now quit their cover, pointed north and let fly, firing at will. The enemy armor ran.

But Bren was watching his other tanks moving in the direct assault. He saw Brill's force overrun the strong point and then swerve and too quickly pivot toward the reservoir. Instead of circling southeastward and coming up on the rear of the fortified hill, the tanks were advancing directly against its face, on the same line which the armored infantry was supposed to take.

The tankers went wrong because they hadn't seen the ground. Bren had reconnoitered it and then briefed them. But obviously he had failed to make things clear. Too late now to recall them, Bren had a suspense-filled five minutes that dragged like an hour while he awaited the result.

When next he heard from his tanks on radio, Brill was screaming, "Where's the infantry? Where's the infantry?" Bren didn't tell him that Brill had fouled the attack plan and botched the timing. He said, "You'll soon get it."

Brill continued, "I'm wounded. One platoon leader got his head shot off. I've lost about seven tanks by direct hits." That meant half his force was already gone.

It was approximately correct.

Five wounded and one dead was the count as of that moment. But there had been some luck. One tank had been three times penetrated without anyone getting hurt. Six other tanks had either become ditched or knocked out. Survivors of the seven crews had scrambled out with their weapons and gone chasing after Brill.

Bren yelled back, "Histaer! Histaer! Kadima! Kadima! [assault, go] and the infantry will get up to you."

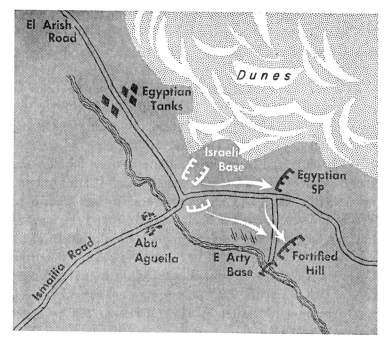

BREN'S ATTACK

Brill came back with: "I will, but you get it up here."

That ended their talk during the fight, not because radio failed, but because Brill became too busy.

Bren then did two things. First, he yelled on radio to Captain Sason to get the armored infantry on its way. Still unnerved from the shot in the back which had killed the half-track, the armored infantry was hardly in hand.

Sason said, "My men are jumpy. They don't like it. But we're on our way."

Bren said, "Well, I don't like it either." Then he watched them start. They got off, he thought, at an angle which was likely to carry them directly into the line of supporting fire from their own tanks on the sand hill.

Bren had sent his S-3 (operations officer) to that spot just to be sure that the fire and movement of the battalion would stay co-ordinated. Now he got Lieutenant Abramovitch on radio, saying, "Suspend all firing!" He felt sure it was as good as done.

However, Abramovitch was having a problem of which he said nothing to Bren. His own radio connecting with the two tank platoons had been hit and killed. So he quit his CP and ran around from tank to tank carrying the message.

What impressed Bren above all else in these minutes was that the canopy of red fire from enemy tracers seemed to build up until the battlefield foreground was brighter than ever. Yet far forward, where the field was dark around the fortified hill, his own and the enemy people were already so close-joined that he could not tell by the gun flashes one side from the other. More than the distant rumble, the weird luminosity right at hand and the rush of flaming shell toward him almost overpowered the senses. He said aloud, "No force can endure this."

So he called Abramovitch again to tell him to throw his two platoons of tanks into the assault. To his utter astonishment a woman's voice answered the call.

Israel's pet name for the woman in uniform is the Hebrew word for "charm." This Charm was nineteen-year-old Rosie Lahar, who had managed to get up front because Bren had forgotten that she belonged to the battalion.

Rosie was cool as ice. She said, "Adolf Abramovitch is out making contact with the tanks." It didn't occur to Bren to tell Rosie to recall Adolf; he thought only that no time was to be lost, and because of Adolf's absence, Rosie was *de facto* in command.

He said, "I want you to order the two platoons to assault on the shortest line."

She said, "I'll do it. I'm already in touch with one platoon and will get to the other."

By this time all of Sason's half-tracks were rolling and about ready to make the turn off the main road, headed toward the reservoir. It occurred to Bren that he had nothing left to command. What remained to him was to board his own half-track and race to join Sason's column. He overtook Sason while the tail of the two-platoon column was still rounding the pivot.

Came then another unexpected jar. Brill's few tanks were already in among the positions on the fortified hill, blasting them as fast as they could fire. That made it too hot for the Egyptians manning the destroyers and weapons carriers. They ran to the top of the ridge and retreated in column toward the Ismailia-Beersheba road. So in their relation to the advance of Sason's armored infantry, they were like ships passing in the night two hundred yards apart. But the Egyptians moved north along the crest, while the Israeli drove south along the lower slope. And neither Sason nor Brill saw the enemy movement.

They knew it only when the Egyptian destroyers paused and squared around long enough to fire one broadside. It smashed two of Sason's half-tracks. Before the other half-tracks could return fire the Egyptians were gone.

The half-tracks ran on; now it seemed as safe as any other possible course since the Egyptian destroyers might turn again and close across their rear.

As the lead vehicles came to the limiting fence bounding the enemy works at mid-slope, in a trice all fighting sounds ceased. The Egyptian hill was quiet save for the crackling of fires where its ammunition stores, supply sheds and parked vehicles blazed. Nothing had been torched by Bren's people; they were still in their chariots awaiting the next flare in the battle. But except for the guns, almost everything of value was already burning.

Sason's half-tracks were milling around in circles as if the riders were uncertain what to do. It occurred to Bren then that he had made another blunder: reckoning that daylight would last, he had issued his oral attack order without specifying how forces were to reassemble and reorganize once they had captured the objective. Now that he had the enemy hill, darkness and distance separated him from his own forces, momentarily being made more diffused than confused by their own success.

Here was Brill's voice on the radio again. He said, "My tank, one other and one half-track are on top of the objective. That's all. I can't see anyone else." In hard fact, two others of his Shermans were with him, a few rods away, though he couldn't see them; the rest of his tanks had become ditched or knocked out along the way.

Then Abramovitch's voice cut in. He said, "I got your order to attack from the girl. I did. But I've lost two tanks somewhere." He had indeed. But his lost tanks had simply strayed off the assault course and were marooned among innocent sand hills.

Bren thought for a moment about the unforeseen problem of collecting people in the dark when no one sees and no one can guide on a voice. He said on radio, "You see the fires burning on this hill. Assemble on the one farthest north." Back came questions from all directions. "Which way is north?" "Where are you?" "What is north from where we are sitting?" "Which hill do you mean?"

At that, he gave up, realizing it was a senseless order. The westward facing of the hill had numerous forks. Numerous vehicles had moved into the draws. None of the others had Bren's own perspective.

So he decided that there was no choice but to abandon the objective. Reluctantly, he gave the order: "Everybody get back to the main road."

Arrived there, he found the battalion surgeon already at work. His operating table was the roadbed. Headlights from several half-tracks provided the lighting. About a dozen wounded were waiting for attention.

But Bren knew there were others scattered along the ridge who awaited the litter bearers. Before helping them, he sent a platoon leader and two Shermans along the road leading to Umm Shihan to block it off.

Sason and Brill reported to him at about the same time. To Sason he gave the task of searching the ridge for casualties. They were mostly Sason's men—eleven killed and twenty-seven wounded from the one infantry company.

Individuals kept drifting in while Bren made the assignment, most of them walking. They were begging for help. "Come up and help me rescue my tank. Its O.K. I just got it ditched in a crater." Or the other story: "I got a track shot off; give me a spare and some help and I'll replace it." One half-track driver said, "I kept going till my tank ran dry."

So Bren sent Brill forth to retrieve the stranded half-tracks and carriers, using his own tank to pull. In a few minutes he was reporting to Bren on radio: "I'm about out of fuel. Every tank I have seen is out of ammunition."

Bren called the brigade CP on radio to report his situation. Ben-Ari was not there; he had gone west on a wild-goose chase toward Jebel Libni. But Brigade's S-3 listened to his story. Bren concluded with: "I'm clean out of supply. My trains had better come up quick."

By 2300 hours, Bren had heard the same story from every unit leader. They had counted heads. Everything was accounted for. Not a man or body was missing. He couldn't believe his luck.

All killed and wounded were at once evacuated to the road junction below Dyka Pass. All but nine tanks had been brought back to the main road. There was no point in fooling with these derelicts amid the darkness.

Bren knew that the battalion needed rest. The two platoons

laagered in the dune position at the crossroads had had less strain than anyone else. Covering both the El Arish and Umm Shihan approaches, they would be enough for security; he'd take a chance on any threat coming from the westward, since other friendly forces guarded in that direction. He told his men to get back to Abu Agueila village and pitch camp among the ruined houses. By midnight they were bedded down soundly sleeping, and the whole area was quiet.

Bren couldn't sleep. As keyed up as if he had taken an energy pill, he sat down and wrote an order of the day, just to make his concluding decisions official. It read:

"We will defend through the night.
"The two platoons which didn't assault will guard the area.
"All others will sleep.
"We are out of ammunition and fuel.
"If we get resupply during the night, we will fight again tomorrow.
"If we don't get resupply, we will still try to fight.
"Don't start up a motor.
"Don't fire a shot except to save your life."

At 0200 hours the convoy arrived with the needed supplies. Bren was beginning to droop. Because of his own fatigue, he decided not to awaken the camp. It was wasted consideration. In some manner which he never understood, the word got around. The next thing he knew, all hands had quit the sacks and were out fueling vehicles and loading ammunition. Within the passage of the next hour, the battalion was fully alert and loaded. To Bren's mind, this was the great miracle of the day.

At 0300 hours he heard sounds of battle from the direction of Umm Gataf. At that his heart leaped up. He figured help was coming to him from the eastward. He didn't know that another Israeli brigade, staging a night attack there, was already in recoil. So he decided that he would mount and ride immediately to the sound of the guns.

By 0330 hours, the battalion was again attacking. Brill's tank company went north to attack the strong point where the fifteen enemy T-34's nested on the road to El Arish.

Bren deployed the others across the main highway to Israel, with his left flank on the road and his right flank moving toward the ridge which he had attacked after sundown. He intended to advance with his two companies to the high ground just short of the Umm Shihan trenches.

But unexpected fire came from his right. The Egyptians had returned to the reservoir position. So for another hour his armored infantry had to engage, first to neutralize the hill, then to mop it up.

By the end of the local skirmish, he had learned that the enemy still held the two main ridges in strength. There remained no alternative to standing steady. Bren's own force had become badly crippled. There were too few men, too few machines, to think of assaulting Umm Shihan.

There followed one day of rest, except for the maintenance people within the battalion, who began their recovery task. In the end, they had all but two of the Shermans operating again before Bren withdrew from Abu Agueila to take up the guarding of Mitla Pass.

Prior to the campaign, it was Israel Army doctrine that tanks should not be used in the direct assault because they were too few, too precious.

War's necessity decreed otherwise. And so the book came to be rewritten.

9...Slightly Overextended

WHILE Bren was putting Task Force B against Abu Agueila, his brigade commander, Ben-Ari, had become a road runner trying to co-ordinate the actions in a widely separated three-ring circus.

Task Force C had moved that same morning southward against Bir Hasne and had captured it by 0900 hours. Defending it was an Egyptian scout company, twelve jeeps, twelve machine guns. The object at Bir Hasne was to put some friendly armor between the Egyptian tank concentrations along the Ismailia road and the open flank of Sharon's Brigade, thereby easing his worry.

Unhappily, after Bir Hasne fell, no word of it passed to Sharon. The oversight must be charged to the High Command. It was manipulating Sharon's Brigade directly, insofar as any manipulation was necessary, owing to the fact that resupply by air was a High Command responsibility.

While Bren staged the assault on Abu Agueila village, which he was to remember chiefly for the overkilling of one Egyptian canvas tent by an ardent company commander, Force A blocked to the westward near where the main road meets the trail coming down from Dyka Pass.

Just before noon, Ben-Ari got a radio message relayed from an observation plane that the Egyptian First Armored Brigade was already at Bir Hamm and rapidly moving eastward. That proved to be latrine rumor. The main Egyptian tank concentration stayed fast at Bir Gifgafa. But anyway, Ben-Ari believed it.

So he sent forth Task Force A to Jebel Libni, there to rig an ambush just off the main road. Force C was told at the same time to pare off a few tanks to guard Bir Hasne, rush north and form a tank park five miles south of the spot designated for the ambush. Ben-Ari planned to use C for his Sunday punch if the enemy came on.

They both started, and by midafternoon Task Force A had reached the designated ground. Hardly thirty minutes later, Ben-Ari, who had stayed at the crossroads west of Abu Agueila with his reccy company, got word that it was all a mistake. The Israeli air had hunted down the Egyptian tank brigade, found it at Bir Gifgafa and hit it hard. In consequence, the enemy would probably not come on.

But having sent the two teams westward, Ben-Ari decided to leave them there, simply guarding for the moment, while Bren continued his squeeze against the reservoir. In late afternoon, the reccy company was advanced to Bir Hamm and found it empty. The enemy had abandoned his main jet base in Sinai without firing a shot in its defense. So Task Force A was put through Bir Hamm and then bivouacked ten miles to the westward, having traveled seventy-six miles in twenty-four hours. Task Force C laagered to the south of Jebel Libni, and Ben-Ari joined it there during the night.

At dawn, Force A and the reccy company moved on westward. That noon, near Bir Dalim, they collided with an Egyptian rear guard—one battalion of T-34 tanks. In a running fight, Force A captured eight good tanks and burned out three others, without itself losing a tank or a man. Israeli drivers took over the five captured tanks, and they rode thereafter with the column, along with ten Russian-built armored personnel carriers also captured.

By the end of this hit-and-miss engagement, in which the

BEN-ARI'S OPERATIONS

Egyptians had tried to escape westward, Force A had foundered, its tanks run dry of gas. They stayed there, fuelless, for five hours, deep in enemy country. Night so found them. Still, their situation did not worry Ben-Ari. Having heard that the main Egyptian force wasn't leaving Bir Gifgafa, he told his men to take the risk. Around midnight, a truck carrying fuel got up to them, coming over the road from the Dyka Pass. Because of Sharon's needs, there was not enough air resupply capacity to stretch this far.

At 0900 hours on the next morning, Ben-Ari got a radio message that the Egyptian First Armored Brigade was moving southward along the big wadi, el Hegayib, which starts near Parker's Memorial and plays out in the northwest Sinai desert. Midway, it runs past Bir Gifgafa.

So he sent Force C riding hard back to Bir Hasne as a counter. While the Egyptian brigade of medium T-34's drove up the wadi, the Israeli battalion of light tanks would move directly down it. There would be hell to pay if they collided head-on in the center of the wadi, with no way out. Once again little David was playing big with pebbles.

But getting to Bir Hasne was easier said than done. The fifty-mile trail through the Dyka Pass was a washboard of upended boulders and churned sand, made all but impassable by the shuttling of tanks. A staff car could not get more than three yards along it without being stopped by spinning wheels which found no traction. It took the Shermans of Force C all day to reach Bir Hasne.

Twilight was around them when they entered the far end of the wadi. By that time Ben-Ari, who had stayed with the force at Jebel Libni, was intercepting messages from the Egyptian who led the brigade advancing up the wadi. The first signal read: "Am in heavy sand. Cannot move. Must have reinforcements." He got his answer, from Bir Gifgafa or some more rearward base (the source is unknown): "Your reinforcement is coming." The Egyptian then messaged: "I don't need encouragement. I need air support. I want to get out of Sinai."

Though the Egyptian was still in the wadi when dark fell, Ben-Ari knew from intercepts that he had sent Force C on another sterile mission. The Egyptian would retire from the wadi as rapidly as he could get his tanks turned. So Ben-Ari radioed his people at Bir Hasne to continue on down the wadi and get back to the Ismailia road as quickly as possible. They started at once, having wasted no time reconnoitering the enemy.

That afternoon High Command had signaled him that another armored brigade was coming through and would be under his command. Its task was to capture Bir Lafham on the following day. Ben-Ari directed it to move via the Dyka Pass to Jebel Libni and take Bir Lafham by 1000 hours on Friday. He was wasting his time. The brigade did as ordered, reaching Bir Lafham at the appointed hour, by which time the fighting in northern Sinai was already over.

On Thursday night, 1 November, soon after he had messaged Force C to return, he got this word on radio from the Israeli Air Force: "Seventy enemy tanks on position at Bir Gifgafa."

Between Forces A and C, provided C got back to him in time, he would have thirty-five Shermans and AMX's available by sunup. The numerical odds and weight of metal considered, it seemed reckless to attack. Still, he counted on the fact that Egyptians, as he knew them, would always handle armor weakly in battle. He decided that his two teams, though separated, would stay in movement so as to attack at dawn. Force A would drive straight west along the road to Ismailia. Force C would continue bumping north along the boulder-strewn wadi. With luck, these two angles of advance should cross soon after first light in line of sight of Bir Gifgafa, where the enemy was supposed to be concentrated.

That was how it worked out, except that the Egyptian brigade was already in flight toward the Canal. It was sixty miles to Suez. Ben-Ari's two teams raced in pursuit, the AMX's showing their superior road speed. Within one hour they made contact. There ensued a running fight between the Egyptian rear guard and the Israeli front-runners which lasted all the way to the ditch. Gasoline had come up to the brigade front via the road, Ben-Ari's own service trucks bringing it.

More tanks were captured, more guns, more trains and more prisoners. Ben-Ari didn't bother with the count. He was alternately moving in his command half-track with Force A and Force C while using a Piper Cub so that he could spend a few minutes occasionally with Bren at Abu Agueila.

While Ben-Ari had gathered his two forward teams to launch the blow against Bir Gifgafa, where was situated the other Egyptian jet base in Sinai, the enemy still held the two heavily fortified ridges east of Abu Agueila. In the nature of their defensive problem, Bren's people could not patrol very close to them after the daylight hours. Away from the road, the ground was too formidable. Any motorized patrol going via the road invited easy ambush.

On Friday morning, Bren's people awakened early. The countryside all around was strangely quiet. Something had changed, though at first no one sensed exactly what.

Patrols were sent toward Umm Shihan. At first they moved cautiously. Come within range, they still were not fired on. The world stayed silent. So they moved on and into the trenches, seeing no one.

The Egyptians had fled. They had left everything intact in the positions. No guns had been destroyed. Other supplies were untouched. But the water cans were bone dry as if they had been drained hours earlier.

Why this had happened, and whence the enemy had fled, remained a mystery through the early morning.

Meantime Ben-Ari's two forward teams maintained the pursuit toward Suez. At 1600 hours they reached the point ten miles east of the Canal where the chase was halted for political reasons.

During the four days the two forward tank teams had traveled three hundred miles in fighting operations. Ben-Ari, on his half-track, had covered 993 miles in shuttling between his three task forces.

Three water lorries, using wheels, had kept the force supplied. Soldiers were allowed three quarts of water per day. It proved to be enough.

When the fighting stopped, the men were given two days of complete rest. On the third day, they rebounded as vigorous as ever. By that nightfall, all vehicles which could be saved were again operating.

10...Retreat to Doom

WHILE it lasted, the fire fight at Abu Agueila was a fair contest, cleanly conducted, if war is ever clean. Less is to be said for the sequel which accounts for the disappearance of the defending forces. Many of these men had played a hard soldierly part. They deserved a kind fate.

It didn't work out that way. Out of the adroit maneuvering of Colonel Ben-Ari's thin companies and the resulting pressure on the Egyptians manning the two remaining fortified ridges, Umm Shihan and Umm Gataf, came the cruelest incident of the Sinai war.

The wretched aftermath was of Egyptian making, a mass tragedy developing from the stupidity of one commander. Ben-Ari's opponent was not known by name even to many of his own officers. He arrived just before the road was cut at Abu Agueila village, and he took over amid the battle crisis.

Whether through ignorance or from prideful folly, he doomed a large part of his command to the most agonizing of deaths after its members had survived, little hurt, the fire from Ben-Ari's Brigade during the two days it beat against their well-prepared ground.

They were in deep works; the bunkers were thick-walled and stoutly roofed. The Israeli fire came from only a few guns; the range was very long.

Though the defenders were partly enveloped, they were

never in truly desperate straits, except that their water supply ran short during the brief siege. For men in battle no other supply deficiency, with the possible exception of plasma, is more demoralizing.

That pinch must have been all the more tormenting to the Egyptian defenders because, within the cover of the Abu Agueila hedgehog, stood the imposing modern dam of impeccable masonry and handsomely engineered spillways around which Bren Adan's battalion had maneuvered.

The project must have cost a pretty penny. Its object was to store flash-flood water of the El Arish wadi which runs from the mountains south of Abu Agueila to meet the sea at El Arish. But that was an idle dream. Water never came in sufficient amount. The flat ground north of Abu Agueila remains untenanted and desolate.

The startling pile of masonry with every sandstone block intact rises starkly next the Rwafa ridge out of unrelieved desert—an enduring monument to scientific miscalculation. The water line shows that the lake has never been more than four feet deep though the dam was built to impound thirty feet.

Where a lake should be, there is only a flood plain of silt-coated, deeply fissured earth baked hard as adobe. That was what the Egyptians patrolling westward from Umm Shihan saw as their water supply ran low and imminent capture built up around them. There was no possibility of escape by crossing the lake bed and skirting the mountains since Israel's soldiers patrolled the road which descended from Dyka Pass.

There is no well at Abu Agueila. The water to sustain the garrison had to be trucked from the Suez zone. Stocking less than enough to keep the garrison going for at least one week was the irreparable logistical error.

Approximately one brigade had opposed Ben-Ari. Overextended, it was still better concentrated than his own. Besides, it had but one fixed mission—to hold. With the usual attachments, there was one battalion each of infantry, field artillery and tank destroyers. These several arms were spliced more or less evenly together, and the heavy weapons were fired from the same works where the riflemen stood, much as in Napoleonic times.

The works were modern; the weapons deployment was antique. Still, it was typical of Egyptian defense during the Sinai war. One effect was to rob the Abu Agueila hedgehog of mobility in the counterattack, which made almost valueless the unusual depth of the position.

This faulty use of available forces by the Egyptian command has only one explanation in common sense: it is the soundest way to handle troops in war if they are not to be trusted out of sight.

Why the ridges east of Abu Agueila were chosen for the main block, and why they have been used as a strong point since the Romans patrolled this same road, becomes clear to anyone who views the countryside.

Running north from the Umm Shihan and Umm Gataf ridges and extending beyond the horizon almost to the outskirts of El Arish is the broad and Saharan sea of sand dunes. They are far more massive than any dunes in North America and the sand is powder-fine.

So expansive is this billowing sea, so loosely treacherous is its surface, and so completely does it cover the ends of the Umm Shihan and Umm Gataf ridges that nothing may move against Abu Agueila village by going north of the two ridges. That was why Ben-Ari had to take his chances at the Dyka Pass.

Tanks, half-tracks and jeeps cannot enter. Rifle pits cannot be dug. Men cannot march but may only reel across the sand surface. The physical struggle is exhausting and the point of no return is soon reached.

Abu Agueila village itself has no military or human value

except that two roads meet there. It is not a village in the real sense but only a speck on the map. The place consists of one shattered stone house, four mud huts, one outhouse and three crumbled walls.

It is important merely as a name. The ridges east of it are important only because they anchor on the unflankable dunes. Not one shrub or blade of grass interrupts the surface of this shimmering barrier. There is not a handhold anywhere. Its massiveness and immaculate beauty dominate an otherwise monotonous landscape.

More than anything, the dunes shaped the flow of the battle of Abu Agueila and determined its finale. They denied easy entrance to the attackers. They made complete the encirclement of the defenders. Ben-Ari didn't have enough troops to throw a ring around Umm Shihan and Umm Gataf. But where the Israeli circle remained incomplete, the natural enemy was more implacable. Or so it must have seemed to the besieged garrison.

The new Egyptian commander got to Umm Shihan just before Ben-Ari's reccy company cut the road at the intersection north of Dyka Pass. During forty-eight hours of battle, his garrison reacted more strongly than other defenders in Sinai, while its water cans drained low.

On the final night the Egyptian made his homicidal decision. A few stragglers, later captured, told how it had happened. The commander announced to his troops that it was now "every man for himself." All should try to get away northward across the sea of sand. They should strike for El Arish, fifty-two miles away, every mile of the way covered by dunes. The Egyptian hold on the coast was already shattered by then. Still, the men obeyed him.

Of the beginning of this dreadful trek, Ben-Ari's people knew nothing. It got away under cover of the dark. The dune side of the two fortified ridges could not be patrolled by Bren Adan's men and there were no Israeli Pipers scouting the dunes.

So that no warning sign or sound would carry to the besiegers, the Egyptians made no attempt to spike their guns, destroy stores or burn quarters, which were later captured whole. Like Longfellow's Arabs, they silently stole away.

When at last the light was full on the following morning, it was only the silence of the two ridges which bespoke that the bird had flown, only to become snared. By then, it was too late to do anything about it, even in the name of mercy. No vehicle could track after these Egyptians, and any attempt to save the few who might have been rescued singly would have been foolhardy.

Hundreds of blurred footprints in the sand marked the trail which no man afoot dared follow. It was necessary to know where it led. The light planes took off, flying north across the dunes. How the tragedy ended is known from what their observers saw and reported. They witnessed the last scene as from an upper-tier box. Had it been their business to intervene, they still would have been powerless.

They saw masses of men staggering, crawling and reeling around crazily as if drunk or stone-blind.

They saw many of these men fall face forward in the sands, lie still and not rise again. They saw bodies already partly buried by the drift and could not tell whether they were alive or dead.

They saw desert Bedouins stalking the fringes of this pitiful host to prey on those who fell or were too exhausted to resist. Some of the Egyptians had tried to carry along their rifles, which are much prized by the tribesmen. Those who were murdered for their arms, trinkets and clothing were at least spared a worse death from thirst, shock and madness.

Hundreds of men—probably more than were lost in any Sinai battle line—must have fallen victims to the sun, sand and the long desert knives. There were somewhere between twenty-five hundred and three thousand Egyptians defending the Abu Agueila ridges. Ultimately only about seven hundred of them were made prisoners.

There had been no route of escape to Egypt for any of the others. Their path, plight and plot go unmarked. No man may explore where they died.

But there is one kind thing about the dunes. Within a decent interval, they bury deep whom they kill. In this episode, they did not cheat the vultures. The Sinai desert knows only ravens.

11...Plans and Pitfalls

ON Sunday, 28 October, one day before the first of Israel's troops crossed the border, two 32-year-old colonels had heard for the first time that their brigades would draw the main assignment in the invasion of Sinai.

There was no doubt about where the decisive battle would be staged.

Egypt had predetermined the field by concentrating the greater part of those of its forces which were east of Suez within the narrow coastal strip running from El Arish to the city of Gaza.

But the finger pointed to neither of these teeming centers of Palestinian Arab life. Though both were heavily garrisoned by the Egyptian Army, each was a ripe plum which would fall of its own weight, once the heavily fortified zone south of Rahfa was smashed.

Rahfa village is not a prize worth the guarding. Some four thousand people grub for an existence there only because sweet ground water is available in an otherwise parched region. The wells determine its location. The sea, the highway and the railroad are all close to Rahfa. But it touches none of them.

Two factors in geography and one in Middle East politics combined to give Rahfa a wholly undeserved place of importance in military history.

It lies astride the artificial boundary where the Gaza Strip latches onto that part of Sinai which is legitimately Egyptian soil.

To the south and east of Rahfa, forming a natural shield against movement out of the western tip of Israel, is a deep belt of hard earth ridges, firm enough for the basing of trenches, bunkers and other military works. Running to fifty yards in height, the ridges are close enough together to be mutually supporting, and they interrupt, right at the frontier, an otherwise flat and sand-topped desert.

Their presence gave the Rahfa position local defensive strength.

Otherwise, there was not the slightest geographical reason why Egypt should have based there a body of troops and a proportion of firepower, which, in effect, staked the fate of her Army east of Suez on this one field.

There is a natural defense line in Sinai, much to the westward of Rahfa and close enough to the Canal zone to be easily supplied, where a relatively few willing men, helped by mine fields and artillery, might stop an army of armor. Its nodal points are Mitla Pass, Bir Gifgafa and Mazar. Each of these is a fire slot, an extremely narrow defile, made so by the shoulder-to-shoulder alignment of impassable dunes or sharp ridges running from north to south.

In ignoring that line to concentrate forces in the coastal strip with Rahfa as the citadel, Egypt violated the rules of military prudence. Thereby the Army was put in the bag, inviting the pulling of the string. There being no reason in tactics for the position at Rahfa, the alternative explanation to that of military ignorance is that Egypt, as a calculated risk, preferred an offensive, ready-to-spring posture, believing that it would terrorize Israel. To keep its clenched fist right under Israel's nose, irrespective of those considerations which

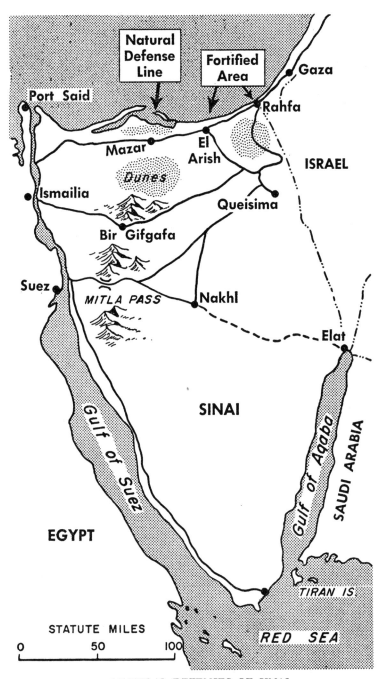

NATURAL DEFENSES OF SINAI

should govern military dispositions, the Egyptian Army stood overextended everywhere throughout Sinai. The price of such folly often comes high.

Viewed in a vacuum, however, Rahfa was a formidable anchor position. It couldn't be turned because of natural obstacles. It had to be attacked directly, and the Egyptians had contrived an ingenious exploitation of its naturally strong ground. There was ample maneuver room for miles to the east of it. But because Rahfa dominated the extreme corner of Israel's frontier, all of this space was like a funnel; attacking troops had to converge as they came within Egyptian gun range. Further than that, the last two leagues were flat and barren, affording no natural protection whatever.

Within the reticulated defensive zone were eighteen fortified hills. Some were of a size to accommodate not more than a platoon. Each was entrenched and bunkered for all-around protection. Within the infantry perimeters were protected bays which shielded the artillery pieces and antitank guns. Each hill was encircled by a belt of concertinas and double-apron wire, and the ground between these fences had been sown with mines. There were no communications trenches between one hill and another.

Among the hills, distributed among the strongest positions, was one battalion of 25-pounders—twenty-four guns. There were also seventeen "Archers." Each position had recently been furnished with an additional, new tank-killing weapon, the Czech-made 105 mm recoilless gun. Extremely short-barreled, it has a maximum effective range against armor at about four hundred yards.

The garrison itself was numerous, if nondescript. Holding the line was the Eighty-seventh Brigade, formed of Palestine Arabs, who are reputedly a cut above the soldiers from the Nile in fighting quality. In reserve, at the large camp which

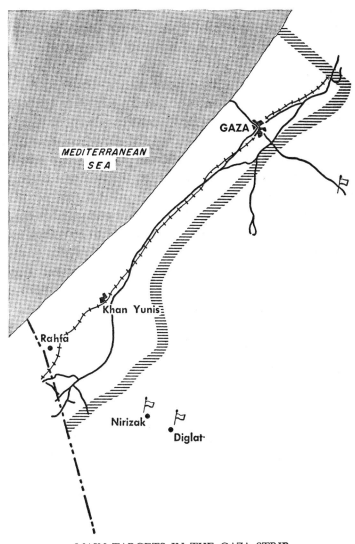

MAIN TARGETS IN THE GAZA STRIP

lay between the fortified zone and Rahfa village, was the Eleventh Egyptian Brigade and headquarters of the Fifth Brigade. A squadron of medium armor was known to be somewhere in the neighborhood. Tanks and artillery were manned by Egyptians.

Hills 34 and 36, on the extreme left of the fortified zone, were its strongest positions. The first is a ridge with the length and thickness of a battleship; its crest stands about fifty feet above the desert floor. Hill 36 has the same height with less bulk. It was garrisoned by a reinforced platoon; there were two rifle companies on Hill 34. Together, the two hills emplaced seventeen antitank guns.

The joint task given the two brigade commanders on 28 October, two days after they were first told to hold their commands in readiness, was to demolish the whole Rahfa position in one night, through direct assault by infantry and armor. That done, the mechanized arm would pursue to the westward. Another brigade would be brought in to mop up enemy forces at Gaza and Khan Yunis following the encirclement.

The battle as a whole in the north was to be managed by Brig. Gen. Chaim Laskov, who later was named the chief of Israel's military forces. The broad design for the operation to reduce Rahfa was of his making and is a measure of his military genius. It was left to the two colonels to improvise catch as catch can the combined tactics best suited to the ground and the time-space problem.

This is according to Israel's system of command, which gives great discretionary power to lower levels during combat. Planning reaches two levels down, but, so doing, is not restrictive. Tasks are firmly stated. But once movement begins, it is left pretty much to the commander on the spot to decide how best to accomplish his mission. The Army plan, as it initiates action by a brigade, specifies the object and outlines the general idea. Thereafter, the lower command works out how things should be done, according to what reconnaissance shows and how the battle flows.

In the Rahfa operation, High Command decided early in the game to delay the battle twenty-four hours beyond the time when it was reckoned the attack could be mounted, not as a safety margin, but in the expectation that the wait would generate panic in the Egyptian defense.

Whether or not it had any such effect, it was a bonus to Cols. Benjamin Givli and Haim Barlev, who, in spite of the added day, were sorely rushed in their planning, the staging forward of the two brigades and the feeling out of the enemy ground.

Barlev and Givli are career soldiers. That is their one likeness. Givli is a sabra, Palestine-born, tall, spare, companionable and a great teller of parlor stories. As to build and face, he could double for Gregory Peck, as even Peck has told him. But he could not play the part with restraint; an animated conversationalist, he thrives on argument. Barlev is the Quiet Man. Grave and gray, seeming older than his years, his manner is curiously self-possessed and urbane. He will talk long and earnestly about any problem which engages his professional interest; otherwise not. The voice stays low and the face unanimated. Barlev was born in Zagreb, Yugoslavia, migrated to Palestine at the age of fifteen, spent three years in high school studying farming, then gave up that dream and stayed a soldier.

Not so, the body of his brigade. Except for five officers and eleven clerks, the armored force in the Rahfa attack was composed throughout of reservists. These civilians were called up two days before Barlev got his mission. The brigade formed as one battalion of Sherman tanks, one battalion of lorried infantry, one company of AMX light tanks and one company of engineers. In each tank command was armored infantry.

Marching by night, taking refresher training in weapons handling and small-unit maneuver by day, the brigade filled forty-eight hours moving from central Israel to the assembly area at the village of Nirizak next to the Egyptian frontier.

Givli's infantry brigade, being on active service, was already in the Nirizak neighborhood. It counted three rifle battalions and one battalion of 120 mm mortars (twelve tubes) along with its attachments, twelve antitank guns.

From air photos and other intelligence sources, the brigades knew fairly well what lay before them. Between the international boundary and the enemy gun line the sand dunes defined the two possible avenues of approach by motorized forces. Beyond the boundary, running parallel to it and the Egyptian front, thereby effectively insulating the latter from end to end, were two elaborately organized mine fields.

Each band was about fifty yards wide by eleven miles long. Over that distance, each had been closely sown with British-made antipersonnel mines and Czech-made, plastic antitank mines. The worked-over appearance of the ground showed that it had been prepared, though there were no telltale fences to define the limits.

Israel's High Command did not know this ugly picture until 28 October. Air reconnaissance was not permitted past the frontier prior to that time. Givli and Barlev got their air photos of the general position one day later. They revealed what the otherwise vigilant line of Army observation posts along the western frontier had somehow missed.

The Army had no magnetic mine detectors, which wouldn't have smelled out the plastic charges, anyhow. The two brigades had to devise their antimine procedures on the spur of the moment. To Givli, it was clear that the mine sweeping would have to be done, but that it could not await the battle.

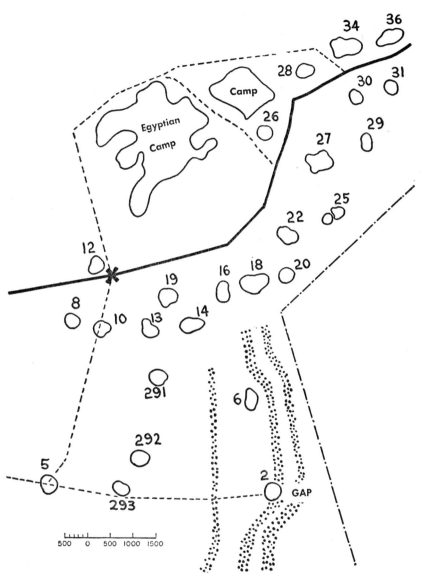

MINEFIELDS AND THE RAHFA POSITIONS

It would be tedious work. A gap would have to be cut by prodding the ground inch by inch with metal stakes. The men were too green to risk that it could be done while the battle line was moving up.

How the burden of the attack was to be shared was more easily decided. The infantry brigade would assault due west through the Egyptian works. On breaking through to open ground, its point would veer north, knock out the fortified hills on that flank and clamp onto the decisive crossroads west of the Rahfa camp. There it would play dustpan to the sweeping of the armored brigade's broom.

There was no finesse in this assignment; it was straight infantry bulldozing, head down. Toward its execution, there had been attached to Givli's Brigade one infantry battalion and one Sherman tank company, the latter out of Barlev's Brigade, as well as two companies of engineers.

The attached engineers had a first duty of cutting the mine fields. The attached troops—all reservists—would have the honor of plowing the longest, deepest furrow and getting to the road intersection which would decide the battle.

Barlev divided his reduced brigade into three teams of armor. He believed that his lorried infantry battalion, with the backing of the artillery, could overrun Hills 34 and 36. He reckoned that soon after the two hills fell, resistance from the Egyptian camp beyond them would collapse.

Therefore, as first drafted, the operations plan envisaged that the brunt of the battle to break down the Rahfa positions would be borne by the infantry throughout one night and the armor would remain relatively inactive until after dawn.

One team—a company of Shermans and a company of infantry in half-tracks—would then advance across Hills 34 and 36 and set up a base on Hills 35 and 37 after circling the enemy camp on the north side.

The second team—another company of Shermans and two of half-tracked infantry—would follow after Givli's advance and mop up as far as the crossroads.

In the third team were a company of AMX's and one of half-tracked infantry. Because of the report that an Egyptian squadron of armor was in the neighborhood, Barlev figured that he might spare one platoon of the light tanks to give some support to the assault by the lorried infantry on Hills 34 and 36.

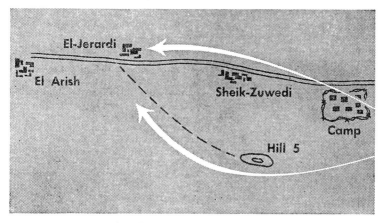

BARLEV'S ALTERNATIVES

But Barlev intended not to risk the AMX's very much. Not only were they to be his reserve during the battle of Rahfa, but he planned to use his light tanks as his right arm —his advance guard—on the quick drive through to El Arish. This second phase of the armored mission consisted of breaking down all Egyptian resistance along the coastal route west of Suez and establishing a defensive block within seven miles of the Canal.

En route to El Arish along the coastal road, the enemy held two fortified places—Sheikh-Zuwedi and El-Jerardi. Each village was protected by a fortified ridge seating a battalion of infantry and at least one battery of artillery. That could be enough to stop the light armor if it took a mauling in the attack on Rahfa. So Barlev played with the idea of a quick shift by which he would send some of the Shermans through on a side road which ran directly west past Hill 5 and joined the main road beyond El-Jerardi.

It could be done only if the other brigade moved through first—and quickly. The point of entry into enemy country, as well as the main avenue by which to advance through it, was already clearly indicated to Givli's infantry. Beyond the two mine fields, a third-rate desert track, well fenced, ran west between the fortified hills, then curved north to the main coastal highway. It formed the intersection called Crossroads 12—the main objective beyond the battlefield. During the wait at Nirizak, air observers saw Egyptian combat vehicles using this road, warranting the conclusion that it wasn't mined. So the infantry would use that route of march.

Its location predetermined where Givli's engineers would have to clear a path through the two mine fields. After dark on the last night before the battle, they moved up to the barrier. There they spent eight hours poking their pointed stakes into the ground. By the end of that time, they had cut three gaps nine yards wide and 150 yards apart through the two fields, and had removed sixty-seven mines.

They might have stayed longer had not machine-gun fire from Hill 6 at last driven them off. One man was missed during the withdrawal. Many hours later his body was found. He had been blown up by a mine.

Otherwise, what was first reported to Givli made it look like an unqualifiedly successful mission. There was, however, one slight demur from the sidelines. While the engineers had been at work, a battalion S-2 had led a small patrol through one of the cleared paths and explored the ground for several hundred yards beyond the second mine field.

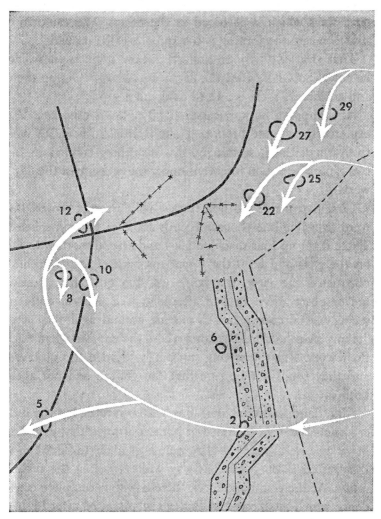

PLANNED ATTACK ON RAHFA FORTIFIED ZONE

He said to Givli, "I am sure that there is a third mine field on a ways which is as broad as the others. We came to a stretch where the footing is too smooth to be natural."

That startled Givli. In another ninety minutes, it would be dawn. So Givli called the engineers, saying, "Get up there and explore. If there is a third field, cut a gap."

At that point, he was reassured. "The S-2 is mistaken. We explored the ground beyond. There is no third field." A relatively small thing, seemingly, this disturbing conflict in the two reports was soon forgotten under the pressure of the day's work.

That day, a rifle platoon from Givli's Brigade moved forward to a line one thousand yards short of the mine fields. There it set up four machine guns and several mortars to fire on the gaps and keep the Egyptians back. Though nothing obstructed the view, the range was too great for effective fire or observation. In late afternoon, the platoon reported seeing several enemy parties moving around as if they were "taking snapshots" of the lanes where the engineers had done their work. But the setting sun partly blinded the observers and they could not be sure that the ground had not again been sown.

All other operational questions had been settled at the final orders conference concluded in Nirizak at noon that day. The brigades were as ready as they were ever likely to be. Mainly, they rested through the late day while awaiting the night's music. At the command level, there was that complete confidence which is reflected in Barlev's words, used after he had talked about how badly machines sometimes respond in war: "As for getting men to do what is wanted, I have never had the problem arise."

12 ... The Puzzling Fight

IMMEDIATELY after the sun sank, the signal was given and the decisive battle of the Sinai campaign got under way.

Before the next sunrise, the two Israeli brigades, who were formed in that corner of the frontier which was dominated by the defenses of Rahfa, expected to smash the power of the Egyptian Army in North Sinai.

It could be done only if the double envelopment by armor and infantry was completed approximately according to schedule. If there was undue delay by the infantry in breaking through the fortified hills, or if the tanks were stopped too long in their swingout northwest against the Egyptian camp, there would be no meeting at the vital crossroads in early morning.

One look at the problem reveals the extraordinary pressure on the two brigades. They must have been filled with a sense of urgency; they should have reacted like men in a rush to face the worst and get it over.

At every other point in Sinai, this Army had attacked pell-mell, as if its individuals followed no other rule than audacity and its columns had no key to victory but sheer momentum.

No real surprise was possible at Rahfa. Here was a heavily fortified position. Its defenders had known for at least thirty-six hours that they were about to be invested. For such a problem as this, the book solution is to bring up the artillery, barrage the ground until wires are cut and the defenders are reeling, then, with the fires still going, attack all along the line in main strength.

Nothing of that kind was intended or tried at Rahfa; characterizing the Israeli attack was a total change of pace, in absolute contrast to operations elsewhere. The one battle which seemed set to start with a hurrah began instead with a whisper.

The plan itself was elementary; the novelty lay in the way that troops were staged forward and into enemy ground, just a few at a time, so that in the foreground there would never be presented to the enemy artillery a broad and obvious target.

What eventuated was a model attack upon a fortified line by infiltration without grace of artillery preparation. There have been other battles in this general pattern in both World Wars. But there are significant points of difference. The main one is that instead of trying for entry via the soft spots, the Israeli attackers moved in directly against the main targets.

Necessity doubtless mothered this invention. The assembly area of the two brigades was perforce remote from the battlefield and the intervening ground was quite flat. Such was the distance (about eighty-five hundred yards) that the heaviest artillery pieces, based approximate to the infantry camp, were at maximum range from the main hills held by the Egyptians. Israel Army cannot afford a prodigal use of artillery; that was another argument for extending the sneak play as far as possible until the moment came when there was no choice but to call on the guns.

So the attack opened inauspiciously with the movement of a relatively few men. One infantry battalion was still at Diglat —only because its legs hadn't stretched far enough that day. It had come ten miles during the afternoon; it still had six miles to march to reach the fight.

Givli's engineers were already forward and flattened within a stroll of the borderline fence. At 1900 hours, under soft starlight, they crossed once more onto enemy soil, reprobed the ground whence the mines had been cleared away the night before; and set the markers to show where the gaps lay. So was completed the first step.

Givli's second-in-command, Lieut. Col. David Carmon, was there to see it done. He is called "Dodik" by everyone, that being the diminutive for David and this being an Army which loves to use nicknames. Dodik was on hand because this was the spot where Givli expected inevitable trouble, mainly because of the planned leapfrogging of his battalions in the ground beyond the two mine fields.

Having marched from Diglat, the first battalion was already at the wire when the engineers completed their check. The two lead companies passed through the mine fields and then moved forward uninterruptedly to within rifle-grenade range of Hills 2 and 6. The Egyptians still hadn't fired or shown by any other sign that they were awake.

The dark ended sooner than the silence. From close behind the enemy hills where the boundary fence turned, two enemy searchlights flashed on, illuminating the whole plain south and east of the Rahfa position. But no outbreak of enemy fire attended this countersurprise; due to the staggered arrival of the assault battalions, the lights at first shone on an empty foreground.

Givli's first battalion had gotten in under the beam and was lying quiet in the shadow of the nearest fortified hills. Its rear companies, leapfrogging those that had come to Hills 2 and 6, crossed the second mine field and continued on, to attack Hills 291 and 292.

Thus far, it was more like a field exercise than like war; the forward companies still had not asked for artillery support or felt need of it.

The rest of the Israeli battle order remained far short of the border, too distant from the searchlights to appreciate their full menace. No one was getting hit and no one was yet crying that the lights over the battlefield made the approach too parlous. This hiatus lasted for more than one hour.

Givli's remaining forces waited to leave Nirizak, having timed their eight-mile advance from that village straight westward to coincide with the march-up of Barlev's armor against the Egyptian left flank. Most of Barlev's men were still sleeping. He had put out an order which split the day evenly, the brigade using the first six hours to get squared away for the battle and the last six hours for total rest.

At 2230 hours, Lieut. Col. Meir Pilavski ("Mouth") led his reinforced battalion out of Nirizak. Just one hour later, its trucks and transports, formed in column, approached the opening in the first mine field. Such was the extra power that had been added to this body of reserve infantry that Pilavski felt certain he would break through on the westward-running axis with little difficulty.

This battalion, which had been attached to Givli out of the brigade called up to police Gaza, and was hence composed of civilian soldiers, had been entrusted with the key mission. To capture the decisive crossroads, it would have to travel farther and do more fighting along the road than any of Givli's "regular" battalions. Because of this work load, it had been souped up almost to the proportions of an independent combat team.

Of organic strength, the battalion had four rifle companies, one support company with six 81 mm mortars and six .30 heavy machine guns, a service company to handle supply, a headquarters company and a platoon of pioneers. Attached to the battalion was one of Barlev's tank companies with twelve Shermans, one reconnaissance platoon mounted on

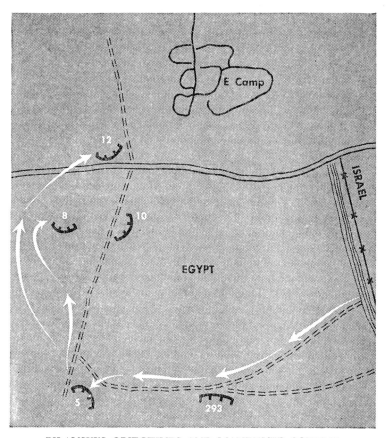

PILAVSKI'S OBJECTIVES AND MANEUVER SCHEME

eight jeeps and one antitank platoon armed with eight 6-pounders. Part of the infantry rode the tanks, some were mounted on half-tracks and the rest came along on trucks.

Pilavski has a singular reputation as the most talkative soldier in Israel. Of that comes the nickname "Mouth," and the Army legend goes that if Pilavski ever dies in battle, the larynx will carry on.

That day, Mouth had talked himself into the easy conviction that if he maneuvered his forces correctly and had any luck, he'd win in a walk by scaring the Egyptians out of their wits. This was a considerable feat in self-persuasion.

The desert track, which his battalion would take on its drive to the westward, was bounded on either side by barbed-wire fences. Though there were fortified hills commanding the road on both sides of it, his advance would hold to this alley. He figured that his riflemen would hardly work up a sweat. The Shermans would move along. Arriving abreast of an enemy hill, they would unload their infantry, get squared around, turn their lights on the Egyptian position, open their sirens and fire a few rounds from the 75 mm guns. (These were modernized Shermans mounting the AMX gun.) If he did not totally paralyze the enemy with his lights, sound effects and a little shelling, the unequal contest could be finished with small arms.

So far, everything had favored Mouth. Whereas the approach to battle is usually more wearing on infantry nerves than combat itself, several good breaks had built higher his already excessive expectations. The Egyptians had turned off their searchlights just as he started from Nirizak, possibly out of discouragement from finding the bag empty. Having completed the march-up in darkness, Mouth congratulated himself on a contrived stealth in movement which had permitted the battalion to reach the sally port unobserved.

Friendly artillery fire was now falling on Hill 2. The infantry company given this objective had asked for a softening-up fire before assaulting it, and Givli had approved. A purely local effect, this was the first flash of steel in the battle. It reminded Mouth that one battalion of 25-pounders was standing by near Nirizak ready to give him direct support, up to six thousand rounds if needed. But he rated that an unlikely contingency. In these waiting moments, right next to the enemy wire, the air was filled less with suspense than with bright wishes.

Givli's other battalions had come along out of Nirizak approximately in stride with Pilavski's column, feeling no rush, since they would attack the hills in the middle ground. Barlev's armor, which would be off to right of them, would not approach the battlefield till well past midnight. There was nothing to be gained, and considerable to be risked, by getting the tanks up prematurely.

The attack in main was set for 0300 hours; it was timed to follow an Israeli air bombardment of the main ridges and the Egyptian camp area. Having tasks elsewhere, the Air Force could not be ready before then.

So far, things had worked out about as preset. Givli's west-moving battalions had been sent along earlier and had managed a first penetration on the sly, without making payment or alerting the enemy. Unless the Egyptians left their works and counterattacked, that gain could not be taken away. Every company that passed through the mine fields meant the winning of more elbowroom for the closing maneuver.

At 2200 hours Barlev's tanks began moving from Nirizak up to their line of departure one and one-half miles east of the international boundary. It was a nine-mile run, not by road, but over fairly firm, gently undulating and unvegetated desert country. They figured to do it in three hours, moving leisurely, but bringing along enough ammunition and fuel to last them the battle, which for the tanks would not end short of El Arish.

At 2300 hours, Givli, having thus far manipulated his deployments from afar back, moved forward to ground just one mile short of the enemy guns, and placed his command post midway between the two axes on which his companies were advancing.

That was when the Egyptian searchlights came on again, catching in their full glare Givli's command vehicles, Pilavski's halted and closed-up column and the companies now advancing to attack the more northern positions. Still, for the moment there was no gunfire loosed against the columns. As Givli's command half-track came to rest, Pilavski called him on radio, saying, "This is unfortunate. The lights have me. Can't you knock them out?"

For several reasons Givli hesitated to comply. Searchlights sound like an easy target, but no other object is more difficult to spot accurately along a battle front at night. They can operate with relative impunity eleven hundred yards or less from weapons which might knock them off with one round if the base could be fixed. Besides that, the fight had not yet opened up. Givli was closer to the searchlight base and more directly in the beam than was Pilavski. Such was the brightness that he could get no impression of their location. He figured it was better to stall a while than to risk bringing on a long-range artillery duel which might limit all movement.

By now Barlev's Brigade was a column in movement approaching the battlefield. The lights swung toward Barlev, and as the beam centered on the armor, the enemy artillery at last let go toward the same target. The fire came in accurately enough. The vehicles scattered into an irregular pattern. But the ground was perfectly flat. Men jumped from the tank hulls and trucks and lay face down in the sand, not trying to dig in. What saved this group was that the countryside was vast and the shellbursts didn't happen to strike flesh or metal.

But the fire volume built steadily upward and Barlev's support batteries went into action, seeking the enemy gun positions rather than the lights. The results were not very helpful. Relief came when the lights shifted elsewhere. The body of the brigade was still far strung-out along the road from Nirizak, the lorried infantry battalion being two miles back from the jump-off line, while the three teams of armor, coming along with their components of half-tracked infantry, were still farther to the rear. The team which closed the column was in fact just leaving Nirizak, though, so far, the advance was proceeding approximately according to plan.

Up front, Givli's companies which had crossed first into enemy country, having negotiated the forward mine field and then turned right to assault the Egyptian outworks, first reported: "We have taken Hill 2 without meeting any resistance." The enemy platoon had scampered away.

Now came another call: "We are on Hill 6." That was quickly corrected with this message: "We went to the wrong hill. Now we are drawing fire from Hill 6. Will you put artillery on it?" It was quickly given—just a few rounds of 25-pounder fire—and hardly had the shells fallen before the company radioed Givli: "We have just captured Hill 6." Still, the Egyptian artillery did not respond to this local nibbling. Why this was so remained an enigma. The enemy troops on perimeter may not have been getting the word back, or the enemy artillery was possibly too uncertain about range and weapons to lay down protective fires. But the Israeli companies already entered upon Egyptian ground saw no sign that the enemy infantry was quitting the entrenched hills.

It puzzled Givli, as any commander in combat must feel puzzled when, having anticipated how the crisis of action will develop, he suddenly finds himself punching in air.

Here the hour was approaching midnight. The first infantry battalion was already amid the enemy works. Pilavski's battalion had arrived at the threshold of the first mine field, and its guides were approaching the nine-yard opening. All of this movement was proceeding under lights, save for the skirmishing of the lead companies taking the forward hills. The formidable array in Pilavski's column must be highly visible to the enemy observation posts, as indeed was Givli's own position.

Still, nothing of importance was happening, and the manner in which the infantry advance had become nakedly exposed only made the lack of a positive response by the enemy seem more ominous. According to plan, there were still three hours to go before the air strike would be laid on and Barlev's armor would roll back the Egyptian left flank. According to the prospect as it had been reasoned that morning at the orders conference, Pilavski's force, having crossed the mine-field barrier, would need those three hours to assault and mop up the fortified hills along the westward axis.

The trouble was that things were going too well. For lack of resistance, the plan was becoming disjointed. Pilavski might run his course and move beyond artillery range before Barlev's armor had moved up to take over its portion of the battle. Barlev was ready, but his assault was in suspense because it was timed to follow the postmidnight air strike against the enemy camp which couldn't be brought in any earlier. The Egyptian artillery was still intact. There was enough well-protected gun power within the rearward hills to smash the mechanized brigade, and it was a cardinal point in Israel Army's doctrine that tanks were too valuable to be unduly risked and wasted.

So passed the uneasy calm before the storm. It was shattered by a thunderous cannonade on the left. During the three hours which followed, the fate of the plan and the maneuvering of the two brigades pivoted largely upon the fortune of one hard-tried battalion.

As is too often the case in battle, the higher levels of command had only a fragmentary view of the action where the unexpected pressure developed. Barlev and Givli were linked to one another by three quite separate nets, through which they were also tied in to General Laskov's task force headquarters at Mir Tahim, two miles east of Nirizak, whence was directed the whole operation against the Egyptian positions from Gaza to El Arish.

The communications channels with few exceptions stayed open, here, as elsewhere in the campaign, the Israeli field radios almost miraculously escaping damage through fire or movement. But for once, the character, Mouth Pilavski, wasn't talking very much. He was the man directly under the gun. His hands were filled. There was too little time for speech. He even forgot to turn on his sirens and he at last remembered his tank lights after the battle was over.

13 ... Deadfall

ISRAEL'S Army knows nothing of antimine tactics, or so claims, having had no experience with the problem before the Sinai war. Lacking a doctrine, it improvised, and some of the results were felicitous.

Western armies use white tape to mark the danger line. It works well enough under the sun. When dark closes down, it scarcely serves as any warning at all, particularly when closed-in tankers are trying to thread a mine field.

Someone in the Israel Army had a much better idea—the marking of the gaps in the two barriers with do-it-yourself vigil lights. Waste tin cans were hooked onto the Egyptian barbed wire so that the candle beam would face toward Mouth's upcoming column without being seen by the enemy.

That made the gap boundaries too clear to be missed. At 2330 hours Mouth reached the portal where the remembrance candles winked, called Brigade and asked, "Shall I cross the mine field now?" He was told that the battalion which had preceded him through the barrier had not yet captured Hill 6, though Hill 2 had fallen.

Then the plain around him grew bright as day. It was something new to be trapped full flare by an enemy searchlight. His men flattened, but the vehicles stood forth in bold silhouette and for six minutes the battalion was under shelling by the Egyptian 25-pounders, going rapid fire. A few men were hit. What saved the others was the phenomenal inaccuracy of the enemy batteries.

The fire lifted for five minutes. Mouth took off and the lead vehicles followed him through the two candle-lit passages marking the mine fields. But so did the enemy shellfire almost immediately. The Egyptian aim was better now. The lead reccy jeep got through the two fields unhurt and continued on. Not so the weapons carrier which rode second.

Fifty yards beyond the barrier, it took a direct hit from a shell, and in the next instant rolled onto and exploded a mine. Hit top and bottom at once, it was twisted full around by the violence of the blow, its hull blazing, its riders destroyed. In the next half-track rode Company C's commander. His driver turned sharp and tried to ride around the inferno. The half-track hit a mine, exploded it and became a fiery wreck.

Landing in the dirt unhurt, the captain yelled to Mouth, "What do I do now?"

Mouth answered, "Get in the next half-track and carry on."

But for the moment, "carry on" meant stand still. No red warning light had flashed in Mouth's brain from the two accidents. He thought of it as bad luck that he had run into a couple of mines casually planted beyond the two well-defined barriers. Even so, he was stopped.

From front to tail the column was under artillery fire. It built up during the several seconds that other vehicles stalled behind the burning hulks. The men jumped from the trucks and dug in for protection. Fortunately the loose sand, which made digging easy, also confined the shellbursts. The enemy was firing only high-explosive rounds. A few foxholes, a few vehicles, took direct hits. Otherwise the force was unscathed in a situation where proximity-fuse fire might have destroyed it.

In this way forty minutes were lost. Mouth rounded up

a few pioneers during the interval. They went forward with their steel prods poking the sands for the bakelite mines.

Twice they went over the ground on both sides of the burning hulls. At last they reported to Mouth: "All clear." By then the enemy artillery had eased off.

Company C put its half-tracks past the wreckage, moving via the left side. Two Sherman tanks followed safely in the wake. But the movement was cautious, each vehicle trying to track exactly after the others. In this way, another thirty minutes were lost.

Then a third Sherman started. Drawn even with the burning weapons carrier, it exploded in flame and roar, having rolled over another mine.

Behind it another Sherman was already in motion and to avoid collision, the driver swung out to the left, straightened and tried to keep going. Even with the first Sherman, it also exploded in flame, with one track knocked off by still another mine. Tracking right behind it, at too close an interval, another command car caught fire. The fiery mass of wrecked

THE FIRE BLOCK

metal now formed a block thirty feet wide and about fifty feet deep.

Again all motion stopped instantly in the now split column. Mouth was close enough to the shock to feel it physically, as if he had taken a hard knock on the head. The pioneers rushed up and resumed their probing of the ground. The Egyptian artillery, given the advantage of an unmistakable aiming point, reopened fire. Men jumped from the trucks and went to the foxholes.

At first Mouth viewed the scene through a mental haze thicker than the smoke. He could not react to anything. The weight of his frustrations had become stupefying.

For the moment, he saw these four blows as unrelieved disaster, for himself as for the command. The plan for the battalion's attack could not work; but if the battalion turned back, the two-brigade movement would go into recoil, and with the collapse of its plan and the night fast going, there would be no chance to conquer Sinai in one quick sweep.

Why it had happened was no less clear. Beyond the two mine fields which the brigade had easily marked from the air photos lay still a third mine field, undetected save by the one officer on patrol who had thought the sand was a bit too smooth. Whether by accident or design, it was the one touch of adroit deception in the whole scheme of Egyptian fortifications. It could possibly explain why the enemy had made no attempt to seal the breaches in the first two fields; his object was to be certain of booby-trapping the brigade.

Mouth thought these things over in a few seconds of time, asking himself, "What's to be done?" Plainly the problem was too big for his level. He needed help—someone else to share the blame, if nothing else. On impulse, while the burning vehicles crackled, he reached for the phone and called the brigade. He described what had happened and asked for a decision.

Back came the word: "Dismount your men, walk them through the mine field and carry on to the objective on foot." Momentarily relieved, Mouth put the phone down, took two or three steps and then quite suddenly realized that the proposed solution was no good.

Givli at the time he answered Mouth could neither see the ground nor give more than fleeting attention to the battalion's problem; right then all of his irons were in the fire. But Mouth, momentarily steadied by the helping hand from above, suddenly saw his own dilemma, from the perspective of the High Command, with crystal clarity, though the sensible answer stayed evasive.

Enemy shells continued to fall around the burning tanks. A few men were getting hit. He complied partway with Givli's suggestion by sending his rifle platoons in file through the ground where the wrecked vehicles had already exploded the mines. But he saw that this led to nothing.

The hour was 0245. The vital crossroads objective was five and one-half miles away. It had to be reached if the fight at Rahfa was to seal off Gaza and open the door to El Arish. The countryside in between was piled high with loose sand. Infantry could not be marched that distance before dawn and still arrive in condition to fight. Besides, he didn't want to attack by day on foot without tanks.

In what followed was a touch of desperation and he didn't ask the brigade to approve it. The lights of his own half-track were turned on full so that men could see what they were doing. Then to the right of where the four vehicles had exploded, stalling the column, a line of pioneers walked slowly forward, prodding the ground every foot of the way. His own half-track, with Mouth aboard, crawled along right at their heels.

Agonizingly slow, this formation moved along fifty, one

hundred, one hundred fifty yards, until at last it was well past the wreckage and through the mine field. There had been no explosion; the pioneers hadn't turned up one mine. But fifteen men had been hit by artillery during the trial passage. Mouth went back to the head of the convoy and said, "Follow me!" Because of the sand, the path of his own half-track was plain to be seen. All other vehicles followed it exactly until certain they were at last in the clear. But it was slow work and the time was 0430 hours when the last tank came through.

Having gone ahead, the rifle platoons were already dug in and inertia had settled on them. It took twenty-five minutes to get them out of the foxholes, load Dog Company aboard the tanks and get the formation squared away again.

Mouth had not waited all this time. The task of clearing the column's tail was left to his second-in-command. Taking his reccy unit, and with his two leading rifle companies mounted on half-tracks, he headed for Hill 5. Just as first light broke, his column passed Hill 293, which had already been captured by the battalion on his flank.

Ten minutes later, the lead platoon of Charley Company charged Hill 5, blew its wire fences with bangalores, and with three tanks serving as a shield, took its trenches in twenty minutes. One half-track was blown up by a mine. A few men were wounded. There were about forty Egyptians on the hill; they fled and Mouth's men made no attempt to pursue or to stop them with fire.

Because of the confusions due to dark and haste, Mouth still wasn't sure that this was Hill 5 when he took it. Suddenly he heard a voice on his radio saying, "Give us artillery on Hill 5." He looked up. Southward three hundred yards a barrage was dropping on another hill mass. He thought at first it was enemy fire; then he concluded it was his own support artillery trying to hit the ground on which he was standing. He yelled on radio, "Stop all fires!" and it was done almost instantly.

The light grew steadily. Now churning around beyond the southward hill he could see a cluster of half-tracks. His own tanks turned that way to fire and he was about to give the word. What stopped him was that as the light increased he saw white X's painted on the half-tracks and knew them for the markings of a friendly battalion which had somehow detoured into the wrong ground.

By happy coincidence, his two rearward companies, led by his second-in-command, arrived just then at Hill 5. One company was moving in badly overloaded trucks. Mouth called on radio to the commander of the nearby battalion on which he had almost fired, saying, "Come to me and bring your half-tracks." It was quickly done. When his colleague arrived, Mouth said, "Now I'd like to have your tracks to load Company A so we can move faster." They were turned over without argument. Israel's soldiers explain that such things are possible for them in battle "because we are all friends."

By now, it was clear to Mouth that the old plan of battalion attack was out the window. Time schedule and the rising sun were pressing against his elbows. Instead of staggering the attack and going at the fortified hills one at a time, he would have to bull through by main strength and awkwardness.

Mouth personally took over Company C and followed the tanks along the road, while his second-in-command maneuvered Company A. At nine hundred yards from Hill 10, the tanks deployed and opened fire on the trench line just to sound out the enemy; Mouth hoped thereby to make the Egyptians reveal their antitank positions before he charged, but they didn't fall for the bait.

So the platoons advanced, under covering fire from the brigade's artillery support while the AMX's also shelled the hill. At five hundred yards, four of the Czech recoilless guns along the enemy rampart opened fire on the array but were silenced before they got off more than ten or so harmless rounds. Every hit on the enemy position could be clearly seen by the moving line. That is one advantage of fighting in clean sand; shell-burst raises no dust to limit observation.

And that was fortunate for Mouth. Already in motion and straining toward Hill 10, he suddenly sensed that the fire coming from Hill 8 was much feebler than Hill 10's, though its crest was at least ten yards higher. At the risk of confusing and scrambling his command by changing direction while in full stride, he gave the order: "Attack Hill 8!"

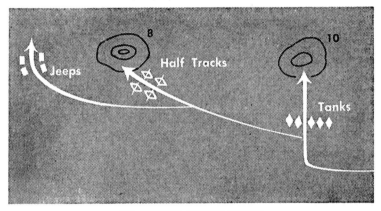

PILAVSKI'S QUICK SHIFT

Company C veered as if already anticipating the switch. Three tanks and one platoon of infantry riding jeeps swung far out to leftward as if to threaten encirclement, and the rest of Company C, riding half-tracks, drove for the rampart by the shortest line. Mouth was with his riflemen as they swarmed into Hill 8's trench. They could see the enemy garrison running down the back slope. His own men did not fire at them. Now he could also see that the garrison on Hill 10 was quitting its ground.

The Israeli tanks confronting Hill 10 had stayed put, one

platoon of Company D still aboard them. There was no need
to radio an order. When they saw Hill 8 fall, the tanks
charged straight into Hill 10, and within less than three minutes the infantrymen were mopping up the trench line.

It was already getting crowded on Hill 8, due to the arrival
of Company A aboard the half-tracks, when at 0800 hours
Mouth called Givli to say that he'd taken the two redoubts.
From the back slope, the AMX's had Hill 12 under fire. But
the enemy there wasn't so easily uprooted. His antitank guns
were answering back and his light mortars were plastering the
fortifications just taken over by Mouth's men.

Because the view from Hill 8 was obstructed, Mouth moved
quickly to Hill 10, taking along one platoon of Company A.
That movement magnetized the Egyptian fire, and when he
reached Hill 10, the mortars, antitank guns and machine guns
on Hill 12 were all banging away at it—the routine consequence of making a flank march in sight of the enemy. One
tank was hit and five infantrymen aboard it were lost.

While Mouth thought about his next move, his tank gunners took over, began shelling Hill 12, at once knocked out two
antitank guns and thereby sparked his decision. He'd charge
immediately. The tanks at Hill 10 would bang straight down
the road in column; if they drove like hell they might make
it before the Egyptians could shift fire. From Hill 8, Companies A and C would advance full speed at the same time,
the first riding straight for the hill one thousand yards away
while the second swung wide leftward on a hook intended to
cut off the enemy line of retreat. If the Egyptian automatic
fire, now concentrating against Hill 10, were to swing back to
the other line and catch the half-tracks of Company C as they
bore straight in, that would be bad. Mouth was guessing that
since the tanks would be riding in the clear and moving on
the most direct line, they would divert bullet fire from the

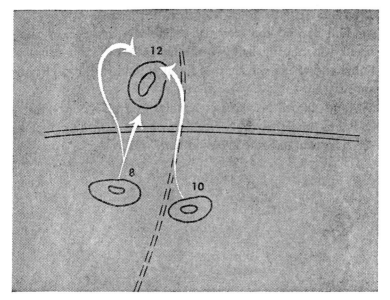

PILAVSKI'S CLOSING MANEUVER

charging infantry. One other movement probably distracting to the enemy fire also cheered him; the main road just short of Hill 12 was by now choked with Egyptian vehicles trying to get away from Rahfa to El Arish.

Both sides of his pincers got off exactly together, moving six hundred yards apart. Resistance held, but so did luck. One tank was blown up crossing the mine field circling Hill 12. After cutting its entanglements with bangalores, Company A crossed the mine field afoot without getting hurt. One man was killed—the only casualty—on entering the trench. The Egyptians lost thirty killed, twenty-eight wounded and forty made prisoner.

Two light tanks were posted on a hill to the westward to guard. The reccy unit was already barreling along the road to El Arish to reconnoiter any possibility of threat from that direction. At 0900 hours Mouth called Brigade to say, "I've got Hill 12 and the crossroads." He was told that Barlev's armor was already halfway through the Egyptian camp at Rahfa and would shortly pass through him. It did so just one hour later.

Mouth spread his three companies over Hills 8, 10 and 12 and then made his final decision of the fighting campaign "to sit down and rest my tired feet."

14 … The Two Brigades

IN his three-hour struggle to break free of the mine fields and get to the crossroads, Pilavski had not set back the planned, final attack by those elements of the two brigades which were still on Israel soil when he crossed the line.

By a paradox, though his column was still wedged tight within the barrier when the clock said 0300—the appointed hour for the general movement—and another ninety minutes passed before the last of his Sherman tanks cleared the mine fields, his predicament was more help than hindrance to the execution of the plan and the maneuvering of the forces set to strike northward.

Mouth's stationary column had attracted the great part of the enemy fire during the several hours when the main body was either moving up or standing on the line of departure, well within range of the Egyptian batteries. Otherwise vulnerable, the tanks and infantry under Barlev gained a partial immunity out of Pilavski's trouble.

There was no way to give him a boost from the rear except as he could be helped by the Israeli artillery. It remained for Pilavski to break through when and as he could. Other forces would stick to their own tasks.

But the block in that direction answered a question in Barlev's mind. He had moved up to the battlefield still undecided whether his main chance of getting the armor to El

Arish lay in the attack northward, which would envelop the Egyptian camp, or in by-passing it to the southward. If the latter course seemed better, he would move the brigade in column on Pilavski's heels as far as Hill 5, then continue westward over a desert track which connected with the main road at El-Jerardi, just east of El Arish.

These options had been left him by General Laskov and he could make his choice according to how the battle developed. When the hour for the attack approached and the

AN ARCHER ON POSITION AT RAHFA

westward axis stayed blocked, the alternative was no longer open; there was no choice but to broaden the battle and put the armor through, after Givli's two northward-moving battalions had broken resistance around Hills 30 and 31.

At 0230 hours, these battalions, drawn up on the line of departure, came under sustained artillery fire by the Egyptian 25-pounders and took their first losses.

That was the appointed time for the Israeli air strike. It didn't arrive. Givli and Barlev heard on radio: "It will be there in twenty minutes." One-half hour later it came in, six jets going at the Egyptian batteries and searchlights with rockets and napalm. They missed the lights, but the enemy operators, frightened away, switched off their lamps and fled.

For two reasons the wait had not been worth while. The delay had spoiled the infantry-armor schedule; it was now impossible to smash all resistance along the fortified line prior to dawn. Too, the two brigades, being at a halt and awaiting the air strike while still more than one mile distant from the Egyptian works, had lost all of the shock advantage which materializes, then swiftly dissolves, in the wake of an air strike. Unless infantry can close within ten minutes, the defender has recovered from his paralysis.

The failure to synchronize the air strike and the advance by ground ruined any such possibility. In this interval, the Egyptian artillery had at last found the soft mark. His own wounded were now passing Givli in large numbers. He called Laskov and said, "Let me go ahead; I must move."

Laskov said, "Then move!"

But casualties before an attack starts invariably become a heavy drag on movement. The able-bodied had jumped from the vehicles and gone flat on the ground. It took time to round them up. In that interim, Givli got the disturbing radio message from Pilavski that his column was wedged tight and forthwith gave him the faintly considered advice to advance on foot.

It was 0340 hours when the armored advance started. Approximately one more hour was lost in crossing the last mile of desert flat to the wire at the international boundary. All this time the Egyptian artillery and antitank guns kept the advancing line under fire, with Givli's lorried and half-track companies, well out ahead of the tanks, drawing the worst of it.

At 0425 hours, Givli heard from the battalion commander driving toward Hill 29: "I can't find the objective. All these hills look alike. We're drawing a lot of heavy mortar and machine-gun fire. Have the artillery put smoke on Hill 29 so I can spot it." But the Israeli artillery had no white phosphorus shell and so it couldn't be done.

Next came the message: "I've found the hill. We're now on the rear of it. But we are blocked by two concertinas which also cover Hill 30. They've turned their fire rearward and we're flat. Have the artillery shell the hill."

It was done. Under cover of the artillery fire, the battalion commander crawled forward and himself cut a gap through the two fences. Some of his troops followed, only to enter upon a mine field. This effort to enter via the back door had already cost sixteen men.

By then another company, still in its half-tracks, was approaching Hill 29 frontally. From the rear of the position, the battalion commander gave the order: "Go straight in!" It did. Forty yards from the position, the lead half-track was blown up by a mortar round which killed the driver and wounded the company commander in the head and stomach. Still conscious, he waved the other half-tracks on.

Almost exactly together, these two forces, from front and rear, jumped down into Hill 29's trenches. But the enemy garrison did not give up easily at this point. It took more than one hour to mop up the position.

Either through rare luck or fast movement, the battalion attacking Hill 25 had escaped the Egyptian barrage unscathed. But the hill made its own problem; instead of being solid, with one set of trenches enclosed by a barrier of mines and barbed wire, it was bifurcated and each half had its own perimeter.

Company A had a twenty-one-year-old leader, Captain Mussa. He was given the left half of the hill as his objective. The wire barrier looked impassable. He asked for 25-pounder fire on the trenches. When it came in, a squad of pioneers crawled forward to cut a gap in the barricade. They were driven back by machine-gun fire from the crest, having lost several men.

So again the youngster called for the artillery. This time, he crawled forward and cut the gap with his own hands. His men followed him and they slugged it out with the enemy in the trenches.

But this night was full of small errors. Company B, which was supposed to take the other half of the hill, somehow got turned around in the dark. It knew its mistake only when the men jumped down into the same trench system which had already been captured by Company A. The chagrin of its captain was the greater because, with his arrival, the machine guns, rifles and one antitank gun on the Egyptian-held half of the hill were now turned against both companies.

Said the twenty-one-year-old, "Don't worry about the mistake. You stay here. My company will take that ground." He led his men forth, again crawled forward and personally cut the gap through the enemy fire; then he took the second position by direct assault. The whole hill was his within a few minutes after dawn.

Elsewhere on this field the tide of battle was running less smoothly. Day was already breaking when the lorried infantry battalion, which was preceding Barlev's armor to break the crust for the latter's advance through the enemy extreme left flank, drew to within six hundred yards of Hills 34 and 36. The trucks had encountered unexpected difficulty in working through the final stretch of sand short of the border.

The Egyptians could see the array plainly now. During the first five minutes that the light grew, what had been random shellfire became a sustained and accurate barrage, dead on target.

It exploded the column. The men jumped from the lorries and went flat. But the floorlike desert offered not one shrub or hummock for protection. Within the space of not more than six minutes, this two-company battalion front lost eleven killed and ninety-six wounded, which should have been enough to paralyze it.

Barlev had moved well ahead of his tanks that he might take more accurate measure of how the infantry was faring. He felt this blast and was convinced it meant for certain that the infantry effort had withered.

Three signalers had been killed; still others had been wounded, and the whole forward system of communications had virtually dissolved. One of the 25-pounder battalions near Nirizak was already pounding away at Hills 34 and 36. Barlev asked that the second battalion join fire on the same targets. Laskov approved. But it did little good. The enemy fire didn't slacken. The Egyptian protection was too good.

It was too late for the men to dig in; if anything was to be saved of the plan, there was no choice but to go forward. What Barlev saw with his own eyes convinced him that the lorried infantry couldn't complete its mission.

Givli called him at that moment, asking, "Can you give me direct help in attacking Hills 22 and 23?"

For some seconds Barlev hesitated, saying to Givli, "It looks as if I must use the armor to take Hills 34 and 36."

What Givli was asking was that Barlev commit everything to the direct assault right then, including the carefully husbanded team of AMX light tanks which was needed for the long run through the fortified dunes to El Arish. That gone, there would be no highly mobile reserve.

While he weighed this risk, several things were going through Barlev's mind. Though the light was growing, within the tanks the gloom still held, and the gunners would have less than a perfect view of targets, especially as they got in close to a fortified slope. So if fire was to be effective, there would be no choice but for the tank commanders to stand in the open turrets and direct the gunfire at point-blank range. They would draw steel as does a magnet.

It took him perhaps twenty seconds to decide. He said to Givli, "I agree and now I'll figure out how to do it."

Barlev's lead tank commander had already moved forward to where the infantry lay prone. Not knowing that, Barlev decided to advance his own command group to the same area, taking along his intelligence, communications and forward air party in the three half-tracks.

At the same time, he dispatched his second-in-command, Lieut. Col. Baruch Barlev (nicknamed "Borka"), to look for the commander of Combat Force A and tell him that he must ready his six Shermans to make a co-ordinated attack with some of Givli's infantry. This was the same tank commander who had already moved up to the ground where the two battered infantry companies were trying vainly to escape the Egyptian artillery fire.

So by this odd mischance, the two Barlevs, a minute or so apart, moved along the same line to the front of battle, "Borka" Barlev looking for a unit, and Haim Barlev thinking through a plan, adding the numbers as he moved along. Their total left him short of what he needed to break the line and run the El Arish mission. If he used the six Shermans to attack Hills 34 and 36 head on, they would not have enough fire and metal left to go into Rahfa, overrun positions at the railway station and quell resistance in the Egyptian camp. The weight of enemy shellfire coming from the two hills told him that the cost would doubtless be excessive. On the other hand, while the thin-hulled AMX team might well do the mop-up job beyond the two hills, without becoming too crippled to make the long run to El Arish, the light armor could certainly not take on Hills 22 and 23 also without becoming spent.

So the thing to do was to send the Shermans on a right

hook which would bring them against Hills 34 and 36 from the rear. Should they succeed there without becoming critically hurt, they could move on down the enemy rear and assist the infantry attacking Hills 22 and 23. The AMX's could wait a little. It would be broad daylight before the main positions were beat down and it became time for the mop up around Rahfa.

That was how he worked it out in his mind as the half-track ran forward. He so advised Givli on radio.

But Barlev had slightly underestimated the two battered rifle companies that he was planning to rescue near Hills 34 and 36. Company B had already lost half its strength and Company D was hardly better off. But neither was demoralized. Aid men were already evacuating the men hardest hit, with the help of some of the walking wounded.

Capt. Ben Eli of Company D had lost all his radios to the artillery fire and was therefore no longer in position to get orders from either the brigade or the battalion. But he reckoned that he had either to continue the attack or stay there and be destroyed. So he moved around among his men, yelling, "Let's go! Follow me. We'll take that hill right ahead."

There were only fifty-nine survivors left. But they got up and followed him, some of them staggering, others starting at a run, then slacking to a slow walk as they grew winded under the burden of their weapons. But it was not an advance by bounds; once started, the remnants of Company D did not stop again to hit the dirt during their charge to the gun line. With the riflemen went what was left of a section of pioneers carrying bangalore torpedoes to blow the enemy wire.

Over in the Company B area, an artillery forward observer had heard Eli yelling to his men. The FO still had his radio and he called his battalion to shell Hill 36, toward which Company D was lurching.

But at the battalion command post this desperate effort went unobserved. Company A was a little farther back in the fight. It received the order: "Assault Hill 36." Meanwhile Borka Barlev had gotten up to Combat Force A and given the order which changed its mission for the day. The column of Shermans was now riding hard for Hill 36, along with its team complement of half-tracked infantry. Not more than six hundred yards behind Company D's stumbling men, the tanks were breathing hard on their necks.

Thus by accident, three quite separate forces were advancing unco-ordinated against the same target.

But it didn't matter. Motion, once restored, gave impulse to the entire field. Company B's remnants arose and spontaneously started for Hill 34. They didn't need an order.

Out of nowhere two planes—Israeli jets—appeared over the battlefield. Not knowing that one of his companies had almost reached that ground, the battalion commander asked Haim Barlev on radio, "Can I have an air strike on Hill 36?" Being equally ignorant of the fact that Company D had arrived at the mine-field fence, Barlev ordered it done.

One jet came in low and doused the hill "right on the button" with napalm and rockets. Indeed, it came in so low that the plane was blown up by one of its own rockets. The pilot bailed out. He landed safely in enemy country, later to be rescued.

While the parachute was still descending, Haim Barlev saw bangalores exploding along a line halfway up Hill 36 and knew for the first time that his infantry had closed on it. By sheer luck, and nothing else, what was left of Company D had escaped a smiting by its own air strike. The men ran on through the gaps cut in the wire by the torpedoes. The Egyptians fled their trenches and no effort was made to stop them.

In the half-light, Haim Barlev had missed also the volun-

tary advance by Company B against Hill 34, and since the
battalion commander hadn't seen it, that piece of information was known to no one. So Barlev ordered the team of
Shermans to swerve from its line of advance toward Hill 36
and attack Hill 34.

The tank commander got the message. But just then the
radio on his command tank went dead. So he returned to his
half-track to relay the order. Borka Barlev rode with him in
that vehicle when the team started moving on Hill 34. They
were second in the column, behind one of the Shermans.

As the half-track, driving southwest, got to within four
hundred yards of the hill, Borka Barlev looked back and saw
the team of AMX's driving hard toward the same target from
the southeast: at the last moment, Haim Barlev had decided
to throw in everything. This was probably the boldest tactical
decision taken in the Sinai campaign.

There was no time for Borka Barlev to think about it. An
artillery shell hit the Sherman ahead, knocking out the tank
and wounding the tank commander. Another shell hit Borka
Barlev's half-track, wounding the commander in the head
without stopping the vehicle. It raced on. Then a second shell
exploded into the vehicle, killing the commander, Lieut. Col.
Ziv Tsafriri, and wounding Borka Barlev around the eyes, so
that he was partly blinded.

Even so, he took over command, and with the half-track
whipping along, the dead commander aboard, the Shermans
drove straight against Hill 34 from the northeast. En route,
the AMX's had paused just long enough to pick up the survivors of Company B and give them a piggyback ride on the
last leg of the charge to the enemy trenches. It was a one-
two punch, the two armored teams closing on the hill right
together. By 0630 hours the thing was finished.

When he got that word, Haim Barlev had already arrived

on Hill 36 to get a view of the situation to the nothward.

He heard, too, that Combat Force A—the Shermans—was finished. Nine of its vehicles, counting tanks and half-tracks, had been knocked out by shellfire, and eight others were badly damaged. The team temporarily could not move, much less fight. It was left to lick its wounds between the two conquered hills. The infantry battalion commander was told to evacuate his casualties and maintain the defensive position.

But it didn't matter too greatly. Givli called Haim Barlev about this time and told him that his infantrymen had at last managed to overrun Hills 25 and 29 and wouldn't need the aid of the armor.

Then Barlev's liaison officer in Givli's camp got on the radio and said, "They're still having a great deal of trouble with Hill 27. I think they could use our help there." The light was now full; that meant that the attacking riflemen might be picked off easily unless they were given heavy gunfire support from close up. It seemed a task suited to the measure of the AMX's, for they have an excellent gun.

So once again the light armor joined the infantry fight, tanks and riflemen tying together while advancing against the enemy, instead of withdrawing briefly to regroup. That pattern had been consistent in the Rahfa battle and it provides the best measure of the fighting quality of Israel's soldiers.

First, the Israeli artillery massed fires against Hill 27. When it stopped, the enemy continued to reply with machine-gun and 81 mm mortar fire. The attack repeated the technique that had worked elsewhere. The hill was taken in twenty minutes.

By the end, Givli had already set his command post on Hill 29. He felt good. The sight of the armor coming over the ridges and taking the enemy works by headlong assault had given him the "greatest moments of a lifetime." His part of the operation was finished, except for the smothering of the few Egyptian artillery positions which still continued to fire from the background. The time was 0730 hours.

Barlev and his reserve brigade still had far to go. He ordered Combat Force C—the AMX's—to carry on with its lately assigned task of neutralizing Hills 35 and 37 and the blasting of the enemy camp from the north, where he had expected to use the Shermans. The light tanks rolled right on through, the Egyptians fleeing in front of the gunfire.

About two hours later, the team arrived at Crossroads 12, where Mouth Pilavski's force awaited. That put the advance guard (the AMX's) in the planned position when the company of Shermans which had been with Pilavski was returned to its own fold. The column immediately began barreling down the coastal highway toward El Arish.

At the first fortified position along the road—Sheikh-Zuwedi —the enemy battalion bolted, though it was well entrenched on a dominating sand hill which enfiladed the only approach.

El-Jerardi was not so easy. From the fortified hill which flanked the highway east of the village, one artillery battery and several antitank guns opened fire on the advance guard. The leading AMX platoon swung out to the south and, coming up on the rear of the hill, drove off the gunners and captured four AT guns. But because the face of the hill confronting the road was a steep bluff, the tanks couldn't get at the Egyptian infantry company which was defending it from within heavily timbered bunkers. Haim Barlev, coming along the highway with the second AMX platoon, figured he could end it in a face-to-face duel, until the tank commander told him, "Too bad, but we're out of ammunition."

It was time to pull back a little. During the halt some of the Shermans caught up. The AMX's which had taken the hilltop also pulled back; they had a few rounds left. While

Barlev was thinking of how to use the Shermans, six Israeli jets struck the hill with rockets and napalm, killing six more AT guns. Though the enemy fire grew feebler, there were still twelve live artillery pieces working from the hill when the Shermans started out.

Again the indirect approach was tried. It proved more costly than was expected. In this maneuver, two Shermans were hit, three men were killed and ten were wounded.

With their fuel tanks running dry, and several of the guns empty, the AMX's made just a pass at closing on the hill from in front. It was enough; the Egyptians ran for the dunes and Barlev's men let them escape.

Somewhere coming along the highway from Rahfa was a fuel tanker and an ammunition-loaded truck. But it would take ninety minutes to refuel; and the AMX crews, in their terribly cramped compartments, had been moving and fighting for about fifteen hours.

Barlev decided to leave them behind and go on, using the few Shermans as an advance guard. This weak-armed gesture, courageous or foolhardy, ended five miles east of El Arish.

At that point from north and south the high dunes clamp right down on the highway, making it impossible tank country. While the Shermans threaded this defile, a heavy artillery concentration from batteries at El Arish came in, ranging right on the pavement. The Shermans tried to fan out a little. But the best they could do was plow along through the sand piles in second gear a few yards apart. Making things worse, the setting sun shone directly in the eyes of the tank drivers, almost blinding them.

It had been a mistake. Barlev repaired it by leaving his infantry platoons amid the dunes to block the highway with their half-tracks. The Shermans were pulled back four miles.

Their bivouac built up rapidly during the night. The AMX's and nine more Shermans arrived, as did one battery of 25-pounders and the lorried infantry battalion which had been left on Hills 34 and 36. This battered outfit, not knowing when to quit, had sought special permission to travel west and join the kill. Barlev had already asked that the Air Force be ready to support him at first light.

Having regrouped his tanks in three teams, he issued his order. All of the armor would move out not long after midnight. There is a wide spot in the road, called Nakal Abu Sedd, about three miles short of El Arish. The tanks were to be there, lined up on both sides of the road, at dawn.

The array was formed as ordered. At first light, enemy artillery fire almost found it. The futile barrage lasted just three minutes, ending when the Israeli air strike dropped napalm on the batteries.

It was the last burst of ground fighting in the north. The tanks got on the road immediately. Already an observer in a Piper Cub was saying to Barlev, "El Arish looks pretty empty but I can see hundreds of vehicles moving toward Qantara."

Barlev signaled Air Force, asking, "Will you attack those convoys?"

One team went into El Arish without drawing a shot. Continuing south, it captured the airfield undamaged. The rest of the column moved on along the main highway ten more miles toward Egypt.

There it became blocked temporarily by loot. An odd thing had happened. Israel's jets had strafed alongside the fleeing motorized convoys, shooting bullets into the dunes some yards south of the roadway. But the people bound for Egypt had jumped from the vehicles and sprinted to the seashore, leaving the motors running.

They were still on the beaches when Barlev's column rolled

alongside the abandoned convoys. So the transport was captured whole—385 vehicles, including forty T-34 tanks and sixty armored cars, considerably more shooting power than Barlev commanded.

Then the enemy people came strolling back from the seashore to see how things were going, and walked right into the bag. They yielded without a struggle, possibly because it is Arab wisdom also that one should never place himself between the devil and the sea.

To shepherd this host of prisoners, the Shermans turned about and went into camp at El Arish. The AMX's continued on to Romana, which is twenty miles short of Qantara, reaching it at 1700 hours on 2 November. Nothing which followed that arrival must concern anyone whose interest in the Sinai war is centered on the fighting character of the victor rather than on the charity of world politics toward the vanquished.

15 ... Gaza Fade-out

DUE to Israel's victory at Rahfa, the Egyptian defense at Gaza did a pratfall, unbecoming to its dignity as an Arab metropolis and its place in military history.

What happened there provided the one touch of *opéra bouffe* in an otherwise intensely pressed campaign. As happened to the Philistines, "the house fell upon the lords, and upon all the people that were therein," but without breaking their skins.

Rather late in the day, Israel's High Command assigned one brigade to play a cat-and-mouse game at Gaza. Egypt was supposed to have about six thousand soldiers in garrison there, and such a force cannot be ignored altogether.

But at first, while the Rahfa attack was being mounted, there was no final decision about how the Gaza brigade would be used. It was heads or tails whether to hit the Egyptians all along the Strip at one time or concentrate on the envelopment at the far end and see what befell.

Finally, the brigade which was sent south to nudge Gaza was told to mark time at a distance and "let the Arabs foul up the situation within the city for as long as possible."

The brigade was formed of reservists from the district south of Tel Aviv. It was called up after most of the other brigades had been mobilized. To it was assigned a new commander, thirty-five-year-old Col. Aaron Doron, German-born and German-reared until at the age of seventeen he migrated to Palestine. Doron was about to emplane for school duty in England when he got the task. He knew nothing of the war plan.

Upon summoning Doron, General Dayan was still debating with himself whether the brigade should be used to attack full-scale or merely to contain while the issue at Rahfa was decided.

The brigade formed on Sunday. By nightfall of Monday, 29 October, it had marched to its assembly area along the old road which runs from Gaza to Beersheba. At about that time, Dayan decided that toward Gaza he'd play the waiting game, and so told Doron.

A main doubt about the sufficiency of the two-brigade task force sent against Rahfa must have influenced that decision. For on 31 October, Mouth Pilavski's battalion was taken away from Doron and handed to Givli. Suffice to say that the result justified the calculation.

During the two-day wait, Doron's staff continued to hug the illusion that the brigade would attack Gaza while the enemy defenses were still solid all along the Strip. Three beautiful operations plans, covering all the possibilities, were drafted and put before Doron. He sprinkled no cold water on the hopes of his staff, figuring that the field practice would be good for his officers.

Though the brigade headquarters continued to sit on one spot, the rifle companies became increasingly occupied with the dispatch of nightlong ambush patrols into the sand ridges south of the Gaza Strip. Here was another eccentricity of the Egyptian enemy. Acting as if they did not know that a full-scale war was developing and that the Negev was now alive with troops itching to fire, the Egyptians continued to send fedayeen raiders over the border in greater numbers than ever. They walked rabbitlike into the trap.

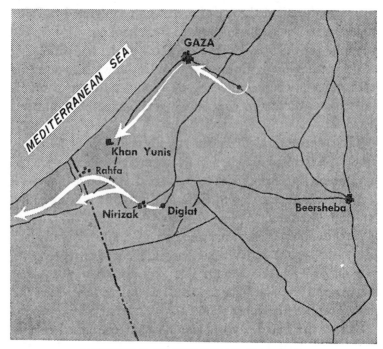

MANEUVER IN THE DECISIVE BATTLE

By the early hours of 1 November, these prowlers were coming in such numbers as to warrant a suspicion that they were innocents trying to escape a battle for Gaza. Doron's whole Second Battalion was split into about thirty patrols and put on ambush duty. Otherwise, the brigade simply rocked along, awaiting the outcome at Rahfa.

Late that afternoon Doron felt better. Higher headquarters called him, saying, "We're sending a combat patrol of armor into the Strip tomorrow morning when you feel ready; it will be under your command." The commander of the tank company arrived within one hour thereafter. He got there just in time to hear that another call coming from above had canceled the order. The tanks were still somewhere on the road, following after him.

At midnight, Doron received another order: he was to move with his entire force into Gaza "at some time in the morning." He answered, "I'll attack with the brigade at dawn."

Thereby he promised too much. The Second Battalion was still distant in the hills, with its manpower split into patrols and far scattered. The tank company hadn't yet arrived.

As the hour came, so did the tanks. Besides the armor, he had two companies of infantry, mounted in half-tracks. This is the force that was put on the Gaza road.

South of Gaza, along the ancient highway which connects with the coastal road east of the Gaza wadi, were two well-entrenched ridges, Hills 125 and 122. They were held by elements of the Palestine Eighth Division in strength somewhat

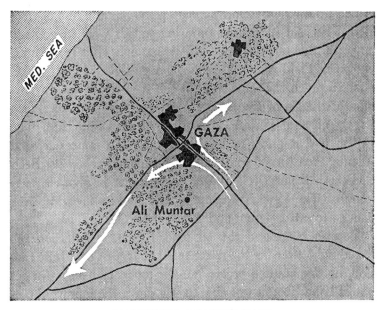

MANEUVER AGAINST GAZA

less than a brigade. Doron couldn't be sure whether the enemy would still try to defend this high ground, now that all Egyptian force within the Strip had become netted through the victory at Rahfa.

He decided to feel out intentions at Hill 125 a bit cautiously. The tanks moved up and shelled it from the road, supported by barrage fire from a 120 mm mortar battalion. It was a full-length try; tank gunners and mortarmen poured it on as fast as they could for twenty minutes.

To everyone's surprise, the enemy batteries on the hill didn't quit. But the gunners must have been panicky; their return fire came nowhere near the target. So the infantry half-tracks charged the bunker line, sprayed it with machine guns as they raced uphill and moved on over the crest, still without having silenced the resistance.

At that point, the Second Battalion reached the scene, unloaded from its buses and walked up the hill as a line of riflemen. That did it. By the time the squads were in grenade range of the bunkers, the hill was quiet. Hill 122—better known in Field Marshal Allenby's day as Ali Muntar Ridge —fell in much the same way. In the 1914–1918 war, the six-month struggle of the British Army to take Gaza developed largely around Turkish possession of the same hill. The British had it once, relinquished it on the same day, and Allenby then turned southeast on his maneuver against Beer-sheba. Ali Muntar fell to Doron's riflemen in about twenty minutes. The Egyptians manning the bunkers fired just long enough to satisfy honor and then ran for Gaza.

Doron's tanks and the bus-loaded infantry battalion followed right after. As the sweet smell of success overcame caution, no one awaited orders and the movement began to get out of hand. Doron was able to flag down the infantry buses before they had passed the city outskirts. The armor and the half-tracks charged on into the center of Gaza, then for lack of direction, coiled round and round inside the central square.

Quickly, the tangle of tracked vehicles became so tight that no one could move. It stayed that way several hours despite Doron's effort to clear the jam. There were still Egyptian tanks in Gaza—more than Doron had at hand—and he could see them moving about in the city streets while his own force was stuck fast. Tied to his situation, anxious lest one volley might explode it, Doron was given grace. The enemy tanks didn't fire.

Within the Egyptian headquarters during these hours was being staged an extraordinary scene, unknown to Doron. Twenty members of the United Nations Mixed Armistice Commission had already quit Gaza to go aboard the SS *Cambria* which was standing offshore from this harborless port. The twenty-first member—Lieut. Col. R. S. Bayard, USA— decided to stick it, conceiving it his duty to arrange a local peace when further bloodshed could serve no military object. Bayard talked on and on to the senior Egyptian present, Major General Digany, telling him that the circumstances justified nothing but surrender.

Digany objected. He said that his men wouldn't obey the order; he feared that any officer attempting to pass the word might be torn apart. It was possibly a higher estimate of the Arab will to do or die than the facts warranted.

Doron heard only that an armistice powwow of some kind was proceeding in the enemy camp. Workers for UNRWA at the Gaza refugee center brought him the rumor that the Egyptians would quit at noontime.

Trying to rush things a bit, Doron extricated two tanks and two half-tracks from the tangle in the square and told them to ride as a patrol to Government House and demonstrate outside. The patrol moved one block. Then a burst of machine-gun fire from a rooftop killed its leader. The fire was not returned. Doron called the patrol back. He didn't want a fight in Gaza.

Noon was at hand. Still arguing with Digany, Bayard was becoming exasperated. Pointing to the *Cambria*, he said, "You see that ship out there. Either you will cease fire now, or I'll leave you and go aboard."

The innocuous bluff worked. Digany couldn't stand the thought of continuing an almost bloodless fight if it was to cost him his last peacemaker. At 1330 hours the Egyptian ran up the white flag and dispatched a number of his juniors to carry the message to the outposts that the fight was over. Doron wasn't there to see it. At least another hour passed before some UN functionary brought him the welcome word that Digany had tossed in the towel.

"Return and tell him," said Doron, "that he has ten minutes to come here and say so." The ultimatum was all bark and no bite. Digany took his time, dressed in his best uniform, and it was quite a while later that he arrived unaccompanied. No immortal words were passed at this conference. Doron told Digany he wouldn't believe in the surrender until what Digany said was confirmed by the tactical officer actually commanding the garrison. It was at last done to Doron's satisfaction.

But the ceasefire hardly cleared the situation of its ambiguity. Having won Gaza, Doron still couldn't possess it. There was need for his forces to spread out through the city and police it; the Arab mob was already pillaging the government buildings left unguarded. About this, Doron could see little and do less. For operational reasons, the brigade had to be kept concentrated not too far from the coastal highway. Through what was left of the afternoon, its men were busy refueling the vehicles and cleaning their weapons.

The peculiar spectacle which was Gaza in its hour of surrender was seen through the eyes of a party of United States naval officers that had come ashore to evacuate neutrals. These startled observers missed the frenzied mob scenes but saw much more which made their eyes pop.

Even before Doron's Brigade had entered the city, Egyptian soldiers were running around in their underwear and frantically pawing earth. Burying together their rifles and their uniforms, they became, in that way, anonymous. This flight from identity outlasted the day and in large measure succeeded. Before Israel's Army had time to collect the Gaza prisoners, they had assumed the mantle of innocence.

Shortly bonfires were lighted all over Gaza. "Why?" asked one American observer.

"We're burning camel dung and fodder," was the answer. "We can't let that prize fall to the enemy."

The military stores remained untorched. Such details also make the Gaza fight somewhat unusual, though all war is waste except for its surprises.

Around midnight, the brigade cranked up again and took the road to Khan Yunis, which was headquarters of the Palestine Eighth Division. Doron expected to gather in the prize simply by reaching since elsewhere in the north all enemy resistance had ceased. But it didn't work out that way. The approaches to Khan Yunis were well covered by fortified ridges, overmunitioned and banked with antitank guns. In a snap-shooting duel which lasted until well past dawn, they had to be forced position by position. In the end, the subduing of the Gaza Strip by Doron's Brigade cost the lives of ten men, with the loss of two tanks and a half-track.

After the shooting ceased, came the haggling. Inside Khan Yunis, Doron confronted a very correct Egyptian commander, Major General Agroudi. He explained that he couldn't possibly surrender his soldiers, nor could any of his subordinates.

"If we told them to quit," said Agroudi, "we might get shot."

To which Doron replied, "Now, look here, you're in command of these troops. So you go right now and tell them what to do."

Which is what he did.

Weeks later, after he was repatriated, Agroudi explained his doubts at Khan Yunis in an interview handsomely exploited by the Cairo press.

"I couldn't believe I was dealing with an army," he said. "They looked exactly like a band of robbers."

16...Gideon and His Men

AFTER Rahfa, Abu Agueila and Mitla Pass, there was still one more round.

But the final stroke of the campaign, which from several points of view might also be rated its most phenomenal military achievement, began almost as an afterthought.

When the brigades were mobilized on Friday, 26 October, two days before the world heard the news, the Ninth Brigade did not expect very much.

It was formed of older reservists from the fields and groves in the north. Its commander through eight years, Col. Avraham Yoffe, who is now in his mid-forties, was almost venerable among Israel's field commanders. Like the brigade, he had taken on years without seeming to age.

Yoffe is another sabra. An Arabic word meaning "prickly pear," "sabra" is the nickname given Israel's sons and daughters who are native to the land. The fruit of the Indian fig cactus is sweet inside but outwardly forbidding to those who would crush it. Whoever first applied the word "sabra" to men had the same idea.

It would have been more appropriate to link Yoffe with the saguaro cactus. He's an eye-filling man, standing well over six feet and weighing about 230 pounds. On an American campus he would have been called "moose" probably. His bulk draws attention because of the grace with which he handles it, just as his mind commands respect despite the fact that Yoffe holds nothing to himself.

No officer in Israel's Army knows more about the business of leading than this one; no other is more articulate or radiates greater good humor. Yoffe would probably wear well in any fighting force on earth while remaining a source of irritation to his own tentmates.

During the War of Independence, he was nicknamed "Gideon." His battalion, which later formed the nucleus of the Ninth Brigade, was called "Gideon's Battalion." On its unit emblem was lettered the quotation: "The sword for God and Gideon."

Yoffe's Brigade was given forty-eight hours to gather itself, draw equipment and then travel to an assembly point at Beer-Yeruham, forty miles southeast of Beersheba, moving only at night. It was transported in whatever commercial trucks were available around Haifa.

The mission from that point would be routine. Using the same trucks, it would cross the Sinai desert to Mitla Pass, following in the wake of Sharon's Brigade.

The brigade did the two hundred miles to Beer-Yeruham. But so many of the civilian trucks broke down en route that it didn't keep to schedule.

The column was still on the road when, forty hours before Sharon's Brigade crossed into enemy country, Yoffe got the first word that the routine mission had been canceled.

Substituted for it was a new task which almost took Yoffe's breath away. The High Command told him that he would prepare the brigade to march overland to the south tip of Sinai by the shortest route, there to break Egyptian resistance at the two fortified bases which dominated Tiran Strait.

Maps and air photos of the region were already being flown to Beer-Yeruham so that Yoffe could determine by which route to move the brigade forward. What was left unmentioned in the High Command's orders to him still required of Yoffe an extraordinary decision, which, according to procedures in most Western armies, should have been their problem.

That was typical. The High Command hadn't overlooked the point. But according to the standards of Israel's General Staff, when a battle commander becomes relatively senior, he should be able to measure operations from the rounded view of a general staff and then strike his own balance. Upper levels shouldn't have to spoon-feed him or lead him by the hand once the task has been stated.

For the brigade, the jump-off point for the advance into the peninsularized part of Sinai was to be Ras-el-Nagb, a fortified enemy post covering a crossroads just over the border from the southern tip of Israel. So it was almost within artillery range of the port of Elat. The High Command said, "Hit from Ras-el-Nagb," but didn't specify how to advance on this first target.

The omission and what came of it are the more striking because the natural answer seemed both easy and inviting. From Beersheba, which is the main base of Israel's Southern Command, a first-class asphalt road runs straight through the Negev to Elat. Going that way, the brigade might have arrived at Ras-el-Nagb almost without exertion.

But to Yoffe's mind, the possible forfeits of such a course more than offset the advantages. Elat is like a goldfish bowl. Egyptian Sinai presses it on the west side. Cheek to jowl with it on the east is the Jordan-owned port of Aqaba, where a British outpost was also seated in 1956. If Yoffe's column took the high road from Beersheba to Elat, the whole world would know about it before the attack could get started.

To a more timid soul, the alternative would have been

unthinkable. It lay in marching the brigade across that same trackless portion of the East Sinai desert which was to strand Colonel Sharon's Brigade. From Kuntilla, the Ninth Brigade would then take a desert road south to Ras-el-Nagb.

Two opposing considerations bore upon this calculation. The run would be all the more strenuous because Sharon's vehicles would have broken down the few tracks. On the other hand, the countryside would be cleared of Egyptians because Sharon would have gone that way.

The almost overwhelming risk was that by daring the Sinai desert's worst for an extra day, Yoffe might founder his brigade physically for the sake of a surprise that would not be more than marginally advantageous.

That was the risk he decided to take. In the end, two reflections bent him that way. Running the brigade via Kuntilla would shake down its parts and uncover the weak spots. Then, too, for the moment time was not pressing. The advance would be like a dry-run exercise, except that the commitment to the approach might also void the operation.

Yoffe's gamble was that the physical powers of his men would be equal to the additional test, which even the High Command would not force on him.

Where nothing about the situation was certain, decisions had to be positive. There is no other consolation than this in an unmeasurable contest with the unknown.

Once at Ras-el-Nagb, the brigade would be launched into terra incognita amid stresses wholly unpredictable. There was no précis in Yoffe's command papers telling him what South Sinai would be like.

He realized somewhat vaguely that over the globe there is no wilder, less hospitable country. Other people had told him that this was its reputation, but they had not been there either. Though the Middle East is filled with wanderers, they do not roam the South Sinai wasteland to identify its features, later to return and tell other men. The cradle of the Ten Commandments is a shunned sector of earth.

This was what gave the adventure its tang. Modern military columns are rarely set up to blaze the trail of exploration. Yoffe's Brigade perforce braced itself to just such a task—and felt the stronger for it.

World maps show the east coastal region of Sinai as having intersecting, if not straight-running, roads. This too is embroidery stitched by map makers who have never been there.

Along that side, there is no coastal road or even a continuous trail. Occasional tracks and vaguely defined trails show where men and animals have moved in centuries past. These traces scallop inland following the dry water courses. They peter out amid the boulders where the wadis end near the divide. Communications in this range are hardly less primitive than when Moses walked through leading the people out of the Wilderness of Sin.

As Yoffe was to learn, South Sinai is a land forsaken by man because it is absolutely waterless, without wells, without running streams. There is shade nowhere at noontime or coolness under a rock. It is a region of knife-edge peaks, sand seas like the familiar Hollywood portrait of Sahara and broad dry washes, canyon-walled.

How to put a modern motorized column across this unsurveyed and ridge-strewn wilderness had never been measured by Israel Army as a staff problem. Yet it involved acute, unprecedented command decisions: What course promised best in an unknown region? How should a fighting column be loaded so that each of its parts would stay self-maintaining? How should the force be organized from front to rear so that protection would be combined with maximum mobility? To these and other main questions there were no ready-made answers.

Amid the strain of going operations, Yoffe had to improvise them. More than all else, he faced a logistical riddle. Yet this soldier is primarily a battle commander and a superb trainer of fighting forces, but not a logistician. Knowing little of the mathematics of movement, he operates by rule of thumb. Other than putting more dependable wheels under the brigade, High Command left it up to Yoffe.

On Monday, 29 October, the brigade was alerted for movement from Beer-Yeruham. The ice and vegetable trucks had done their service. From elsewhere in the Sinai operation, there were driven to the command 104 six-by-six GMC trucks, 32 command cars and weapon carriers, 14 half-tracks and 34 jeeps and three-quarter tonners. This was the total lift.

The column would be fairly long. Yoffe reckoned he must so load and echelon it that both its fighting and supply problems would be solved from the start of the march. Nothing should be shifted en route unless a vehicle broke down wholly. Each party and machine would be supplied for self-sufficiency. In that way, the brigade would try for continuous movement insofar as it was humanly possible.

After coming to his main decisions, Yoffe had just one half-day in which to get the essential work done. He could not be sure that the brigade could even accomplish the journey. What bothered him most was the vexing question of how to conduct a march this strenuous and still have his men get to the Tiran Strait in condition to fight.

Yoffe guessed that if his luck held, he could push the brigade over 240 miles of unknown, unroaded country in about three days. That is a phenomenal rate of advance into enemy country even when the landscape is inviting; it risks the stretching out of forces beyond control by the commander. He had already dismissed that risk as unimportant. Speed was of the essence. In estimating he could do it in three days. Yoffe guided only on his hope and instinct.

On the basis of that calculation, he directed that each vehicle should carry enough fuel for the entire journey and sufficient rations, ammunition and water to sustain its occupants for five days.

Men would sleep and eat while the column moved. There would be occasional comfort stops only. Water needs were reckoned at one gallon per man and per vehicle per day. Water rationing was encharged to officers in each vehicle to prevent water wastage. The word went to troops: "You will not shave or wash until this campaign is over!"

Should a vehicle break down, its party would push it aside and wait. A repair unit would close the column. If repairs could not make the vehicle roadworthy, it would be cannibalized. Stranded men would be picked up by the few trucks running empty.

Ordinarily one GMC six-by-six will haul a platoon. The five-day supply load made that impossible, limited each truck to one half of a platoon and raised fresh questions about how to compose the column.

Present at Beer-Yeruham was much too large a force to be squeezed into the transport which High Command had provided and still satisfy the standard which Yoffe felt essential to mobility. It counted two battalions of infantry, one battalion (twelve guns) of artillery, one battalion of heavy mortars, one platoon of sappers, two Piper Cubs, eight AMX tanks, one battery of antiaircraft artillery, one airstrip unit, an augmented surgical detachment and a communications group from the Israel Navy.

The scaling down of this force, a decision made almost by impulse, may not be a model of its kind, but there are few better examples of taking a high risk to preserve a decisive, if abstract, principle. In a big way, firepower was sacrificed to velocity. Yoffe dropped the AA guns, two batteries of artillery, two of mortars and all of the AMX tanks, which he figured couldn't stay the course anyway. One company was cut away from each infantry battalion. Every clerk, cook and supply man was shaken out of the command, under orders to proceed to Elat and wait. There remained in the brigade only weapons users. So reduced, the brigade counted 1,701 noses, including twenty-six women soldiers and nurses.

How it was organized was no less contemptuous of imaginable dangers.

Yoffe built his advance guard of twelve jeeps, four mortars, one half-tracked infantry company, a few sappers and medics and the air liaison unit.

In the second serial rode Brigade Headquarters (on half-tracks) and one company of infantry. The third serial was formed of one infantry battalion and the eight 120 mm mortars. Fourth, and closing the column, were the remaining infantry, artillery, surgical detachment, etc.

YOFFE'S BRIGADE IN THE BIG WADI

But here was the oddest touch—the advance guard would stay twenty miles ahead of its closest support. The other serials would maintain intervals of several miles. That would lessen the dust. But Yoffe also reckoned that the distances would have a cushioning effect, help overall mobility and make a general block less likely. If, when too greatly compressed, an overland column becomes paralyzed, it is more difficult to tell quickly just where the trouble lies.

Yoffe reckoned the two Piper Cubs could keep all elements apprised of what happened. If any serial got waylaid, the next one would build up on it soon enough. Its own firepower would be sufficient to last until help arrived. But a fight would not otherwise retard the general forward movement. It would continue despite losses. If an ambush occurred and there were casualties, they would be put beside the trail and the serial would carry on. Except for immediate first aid, they would be attended by the surgical unit which closed the column.

This is asking a lot from soldiers, especially when they know beforehand of the stern requirement. Knowing his brigade, Yoffe was confident it would be given. Between leader and led was an unusually intimate relationship. He had been a long time with the brigade. Its nucleus was formed of Yoffe's battalion during the War of Independence. The ranks were from the farms south of Haifa. The officers were old friends and comrades.

In fact, "old" was the word for this brigade. It was formed of reservists, most of them between thirty and thirty-five years. By American standards, men in that age bracket will wear down excessively under the sustained grind of infantry operations; that portion, according to the American view, is fit only for eager youth. Senior commanders like Yoffe in Israel Army hold an opposite view—that thirty-year-olds will endure greater field exertion without sleep and will show greater steadiness under fire.

The merits of this argument aside, Yoffe's extra confidence in the older heads spurred him to the gamble. To the younger commanders of the United States Army who have known battle this will not seem wholly odd. Ask them and they will say that if they must lead youths into combat, a sprinkling of older men for steadiness will double the impact.

Of the prolonged association between brigade and Colonel had come a happy state of mutual trust which Yoffe honored within reasonable command limits. He was taking enough risks with the unknown; there could be no chance-taking on matters fully within his control.

Here is the golden rule of the commander who sits at war as at a poker game. Amid uncertainty about the odds and what strength is hidden on the other side of the table, one must at least be sure about what is in one's own hand. There is no excuse for not knowing.

So it was that, when at first light on 31 October the brigade started moving across the Negev toward the enemy frontier, Yoffe moved to the head of the column. Running through his mind was a saying learned in British Eighth Army operations across North Africa: "It's always the overload that kills you in desert movement." He had set three and one-half tons as the load limit for trucks. Against that figure, he checked each vehicle as it passed. The inspection paid off. Yes, they were trustworthy soldiers, but many of them had sneaked extra ammunition, food and personal supplies aboard, as soldiers ever will. The discard piled high.

Otherwise the start was bright with promise. During the night, while Sharon's men were preparing to clear the Mitla Pass, a two-company task force from Yoffe had made a fast run by road and captured the Egyptian strong point at Ras-el-Nagb.

The door to the South Sinai desert now lay open. But those tidings did not lessen for the brigade the ordeal of manhandling its way across that same stretch of the East Sinai desert which had stranded Sharon's main body at the start. The brigade was eighteen hours getting through the seventy-mile wasteland eastward of Kuntilla. Its motorized serials had moved more slowly than the marching pace of infantry. The brigade had tried to follow in Sharon's prints exactly, which but doubled its exertions. The earlier column had pounded the track to powder and the dust lay knee-deep. It was no use telling himself, Yoffe concluded, that the march had provided enough schooling experience in the testing of vehicles and the resistance of the sand seas to be worth while. He knew before he was two hours along the road that the decision to advance via Kuntilla had been a mistake.

Once arrived at Kuntilla, however, the brigade breathed easier. Ras-el-Nagb lies only thirty miles to the south, and a fairly good desert road connects the two places. Furthermore, time no longer pressed. H-Hour for the brigade's push into South Sinai was being held in suspension, pending the arrival of some of the more northern forces in the Suez zone. Yoffe's undertaking would need help from the Air Force, but for the time being the air was fully occupied helping the ground battle in the north.

At Ras-el-Nagb the brigade got a blessed twenty-four hours of rest. Yoffe had taken over an Egyptian telephone line, and extended it over the border, so that he was directly connected with High Command. On Friday, 2 November, at 0400 hours, he got his call. Dayan was speaking. He said only, "Move off!" and Yoffe moved. This matter-of-factness was typical of an Army which, practicing economy of words, almost taboos written messages.

In what follows, success was already half won because of another gambling decision Yoffe had tentatively taken, with the High Command's blessing, after prolonged study of a seemingly insoluble time-and-space problem.

Yoffe had set three days as the time limit for the march to Sharm-El-Sheikh. Should the advance take longer than that, strategic and political changes might deny him the prize altogether. The target was two hundred miles away in a beeline. But if the brigade followed such tracks as the map indicated were most suitable for motorized travel, the distance would approximately double. In two great loops these primitive trails, which follow the wadi courses, lead away from the coast, and then back to it. Though their zigzag course is clearly indicated on the maps, it is not shown whether the lines intersect somewhere along the watershed of the interior, where the wadis begin. That scarcely mattered to Yoffe. He had already decided that the zigzag pattern was not for the brigade. If he tried to follow it, then the enterprise would be beaten by the wilderness; he realized that well before he set up his five-day supply load.

The alternative was to march the column straight across the base of the longest loop, where the two indirect trails which follow the main wadis converge near Mount Sinai. By taking a branch wadi which cut through the hills much closer to the coast, he could save about one hundred miles, that is, provided he could get through at all. It would mean committing his motorized brigade to a countryside so arid and boulder-strewn as to repel cavalry. He so chose, knowing that the decision would either make him or break him.

Herein lies the unique flavor of this operational problem and its solutions. Rarely does it happen in war that every decision, which may be seen in retrospect as determining the event, is taken before movement begins. Yet that is how this show unfolded. From the moment of departure, Yoffe had it in the bag.

So saying does not minimize the hazard and possible forfeit. Awaiting the brigade at Sinai's south tip were fifteen hundred Egyptians. The enemy garrison was almost numerically equal to Yoffe's strength. The defenders occupied concrete works and deep-dug trenches. If the brigade lost half its energy in battling the harsh countryside, there could be enough power at Sharm-El-Sheikh to destroy it.

What the enemy might do, however, was of less concern to Yoffe than whether his own supply calculations would prove adequate. One small cushion, supplied by Israel's Navy, gave him a margin of safety.

At Elat were five LCM's (landing craft mechanized) which could be used to run hot cargo down the Sinai coast if the brigade foundered close to it. Not enough was known about beach conditions and soundings to be sure the scheme would work.

Weighing thirty tons, with a beam of fifteen feet, an LCM is just large enough to house a light tank, and so constructed as to land the tank dry in smooth water. But it is a slow goer and not meant for the open seas.

These five LCM's had been at Haifa when mobilization began. The decision to shift them to Elat was taken in early morning of 27 October. They went to Beersheba by rail. Several houses had to be cleared from near the rail line to permit their passage. The hauling from Beersheba to Elat was done by trucks regularly used to carry phosphates from the Dead Sea. The LCM's were floated at Elat on 29 October, the same day that Yoffe at Beer-Yeruham wrote his loading plan for the brigade. So Yoffe was protected, or to put it more accurately, the brigade dangled from a shoestring still untested.

17 ... Fatigue and Fire

BY noontime of the first day, the point of the column was
past Ein-el-Furtaga, which is twelve miles inland from
the Gulf of Aqaba, about one third of the distance from Elat
to Sharm-El-Sheikh.

The track for all that distance had followed the Wadi Watir
and for the brigade vehicles the going was not too bad. The
wadi was fairly flat, conveniently broad and surfaced with
heavy gravel more than sand, so that there was little dust.
The temperature that first afternoon was an average of about
86° Fahrenheit. The wheeled convoy had no trouble breathing. Because of the grit, the half-tracks began having trouble
with grease in the rollers, and the flying-in of grease was one
of the first missions given the Pipers.

From Ein-el-Furtaga southward, the way led steadily uphill. The track was boulder-strewn; its margins were almost
obliterated by deep sand. That of itself did not hurt too much
since the base of the track was not wide enough over most of
the distance to support the truck wheels. The half-tracks
bounced along over this proving ground. Men riding the
trucks and command cars had to unload and maneuver their
vehicles up the incline by muscle power. Afoot, ahead of
the first vehicle in the advance guard, the sappers worked as
a clearing crew, sweeping the rocks aside so that drivers would
see which way the track ran.

By nightfall the brigade had advanced an additional six miles. Its pace throughout that night was less than three miles per hour. Still, it labored painfully on through the darkness, and at last, when it seemed that spirit and body could give no more, became stuck tight.

Yoffe by this time was up with his advance guard, which was under command of Lieut. Arik Nachamkain, a thirty-year-old reservist who had lost one eye in the War of Independence. What had happened is best described in Yoffe's own words: "Night is not the best time to look for a short cut in unknown country. That is what I was doing.

"So out of the main wadi, we veered southward to beat our way up a contributory wadi. There we were clunking our way uphill across a field of boulders with no path or star to guide on.

"Suddenly the front vehicles bogged down. We were pointing upward toward a divide at thirty-five hundred feet. Confronting us, blocking us, was a natural phenomenon—a great sand formation which covered both sides of the divide so that the ridge looked snow-capped.

"There were no dunes. Save for great ripples, the face of this sea was fairly smooth. How deep the sand was piled, there was no telling. But the field extended eight miles. Loaded as we were, the way was forbidden."

First, Yoffe ordered his men to rest briefly. He then issued orders. Deflate all tires. Every vehicle hold to the same track marks. Men unload and push. When the vehicle stuck, unload supply and portage it.

Even so, disaster was narrowly averted. To get over those eight miles cost the brigade ten hours. Eight vehicles broke down wholly. As the machines struggled, tanks drained empty at four times the normal rate. Come to the summit, Yoffe took stock and concluded that "my brilliant gas calculations

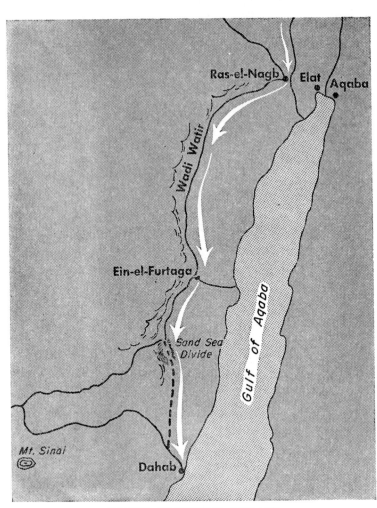

ROUTE OF YOFFE'S BRIGADE

have been shot to hell." From there he radioed the LCM's at Elat: "I must have petrol."

It was easier going downhill, not because the sand was less, but because there was some help from gravity. Once headed out of it, the advance guard made for Dahab, the nearest coastal village at which to keep the rendezvous with the supply moving by sea.

Yoffe stayed behind, astride the sand sea, to supervise the engineering task of levering the brigade over the hump. The exertions of the advance guard had impressed him that this one geographical obstacle was the point of main trial in the undertaking. If the brigade surmounted it, whatever difficulties followed would be overcome. There was one other point: he could catch a little rest while awaiting the upcoming serial.

So as noontime passed on Saturday, the forces of the column and its auxiliary naval supply were far spread. Two LCM's, both loaded with gasoline, were churning through the Gulf halfway to Dahab. The first serial of the brigade's main body was straining against the sand barrier amid the ridge tops. More than twenty miles forward of it, the point of the advance guard was riding, rather than reconnoitering, into Dahab.

Success or fatigue, or the two together, had made its soldiers careless. Though long deserted by its Arab community, Dahab had been made a fortified place by the Egyptian Army. The works were manned only by one section under an officer. It was too little resistance to count, had due caution been exercised. But as it happened, this forlorn detachment fought back and Yoffe's men walked into the trap. In the end the Egyptian squad was wiped out. But three Israelis were killed and six wounded in this brief action. It did not slow Arik Nachamkain's force.

When later in the day Yoffe got to Dahab, the advance

guard was already gone. Arik had left behind the dead and
the critically wounded under the care of a first-aid man. Also,
there was a note from Arik to Yoffe explaining what had
happened. That took the keen edge off the arrival of the two
LCM's at Dahab with the cargo of gasoline.

Out of Dahab, the brigade again tried another short cut,
going toward the Ashira divide which, four thousand feet
above sea level, bumps one shoulder of the Jebel Ashira. This
time the summit was blocked by a mile-long stretch of boulders which choked the terminals of the wadis on both sides of
the divide.

The advance guard was stopped cold and the other serials
shortly compressed behind it. The sappers then took over,
directing the clearing work by the infantry. For about five and
one-half hours on both sides of midnight that Saturday the
heavy labor continued. The path was at last open.

From this last barrier, the route descended to the flat coastal
strip near Maqb. Yoffe had a premonition. The wadi used in
the descent from the Ashira Pass would be the final defile
constricting the brigade's movement. Here, if anywhere, an
Egyptian ambush was to be expected.

The hunch proved right. It was about 0230 hours when
suddenly, not far from the mouth of the wadi, the advance
guard was stopped by rifle and automatic rifle. It was too
dark for the Egyptians to see anything of their targets; they
were simply shooting at noise. The volume was impressive but
the aim was far too high.

But there was no action and no loss. Just like that, the
advance guard went into recoil and, pulling back while sound-
ing the alarm, stopped the whole brigade. Yoffe didn't argue
about the matter. He looked at the men around him and
judged that they were too spent physically to fight. To the
commander, that was warning enough. Two hours' sleep

would make a great difference in the brigade; nature would take care of it. Still in the wadi, with the position of the Egyptians left unscouted, Yoffe directed his men to suspend all activity. The advance guard would resume the attack as soon as possible after first light.

SHARM-EL-SHEIKH'S FORTIFIED RIDGES

Yoffe also slept for about thirty winks. He was awakened by a call on radio. The hour was around 0300. The caller was the Chief of Staff, Dayan. He was flying around in a Dakota directly above the sprawled brigade. That was how he commanded during the Sinai operation. While the fighting was on, he visited every brigade except Sharon's. A familiar figure at the front, he was seen by his own headquarters staff occasionally.

For a moment or two, he and Yoffe double-talked one another to make certain of identification.

One said, "This is Avraham."

The other replied, "I am the father of Yael and the husband of Ruth."

Having named his nearest kin, Dayan ended the sparring. He said, "I'd know your voice anywhere. Now let's get on with it. How are your men?"

Said Yoffe, "They're all O.K. I'd say we are shipshape."

Asked Dayan, "Can you finish this business tomorrow?"

Said Yoffe, "I'm sure of it."

Said Dayan, "Then get moving!" The conversation had lasted only a few minutes. Impressed with the fact that the chief was anxious to conclude the campaign at the earliest possible moment, Yoffe let his men sleep on.

When morning came, the brigade moved again but the enemy was gone.

Thenceforth to Ras-Nasrani the soft-top coastal road ran invitingly flat and relatively straight. This village on the Sinai

TIRAN STRAIT AT RAS-NASRANI

mainland dominates the one narrow passage by which world shipping may enter the Gulf of Aqaba.

The channel hard by Ras-Nasrani is only eight hundred yards across and about one hundred fathoms deep. It is constricted by a chain of coral islets which lies between Ras and Tiran Island. Though on the map the mouth of the Gulf seems to yawn wide open, it is everywhere else choked by reefs and shoals. The linchpin of land-based blockade is not Tiran Island but Ras-Nasrani. Egypt had armed Ras-Nasrani as if to repel a cruiser squadron. Its underground fortress was hewn out of solid rock. Four heavy naval guns pointed seaward covering the approach to the channel. To forbid merchantmen the passage would have required not more than as many machine guns mounted at the same point. Covering the landward approaches to the main fortress was a semicircular, half-mile-deep hedgehog of concrete bunkers and interconnecting trenches, behind a wide belt of wire entanglements interlaced with mine fields. One battalion firmly committed to the defense of this position might well have withstood a division attack, so artillery-resistant were its works.

Yoffe moved up with his advance guard. Ras-Nasrani was to be taken with a rush, despite its fearsome look, the Egyptians not having mined the road. And so it was, though the blow landed in air, the enemy having fled his most formidable position. Nothing is more enigmatic than the Egyptian military mind, to use a term loosely. Two days earlier the commander had heard by radio that a "reconnaissance unit consisting of several tracked vehicles" was headed toward him. Thereupon he had abandoned his citadel and withdrawn its forces to the semiorganized, weakly sited position at Sharm-El-Sheikh to honor the principle of concentration.

The advance guard did not so much as pause for one quick view of the Ras-Nasrani prize. Yoffe's command car kept moving and he waved the others on. The brigade was rolling along now on asphalt pavement. Yoffe intended to maintain the momentum until a first shock blow fell on the outer defenses of the enemy camp. But despite what he had told Dayan in early morning, he did not plan to fight a clean-up action that day.

To hit and then pull up—here again was a novel calculation. The reasoning behind it was elementary. The Egyptian forces were already forewarned and as poised for action as they were ever likely to be. If they were hit and hurt in one spot, the suspension of fighting would serve only further to demoralize them. The brigade, on the other hand, would become rested through the prolonged halt. Once again collected, it would gain that extra confidence which comes of seeing one's own total strength arrayed.

The tactical pause, taken for reasons which relate almost wholly to the spiritual values, is one of the least understood nuances in the art of command. When success appears right at hand, or when troops are in desperate straits, with the road to the rear already closed, the temptation to hit out and keep going builds up almost irresistibly. Students who are interested in this subject cannot do better than to study the decisions of Maj. Gen. Oliver P. Smith in the campaign of the U.S. First Marine Division around the Chosin Reservoir, Korea, which are in every way exemplary. Smith was a master of the inspirational wait.

At noontime on Sunday Yoffe's advance guard broke through the outguard line at Sharm-El-Sheikh and in a brisk action opened the way to the main defenses. Fighting operations were then suspended, and Yoffe waited for the rest of the column to close on the camp. For all hands there was approximately a twelve-hour pause before anything else was done. The day was fair and the breeze from the sea was refreshing.

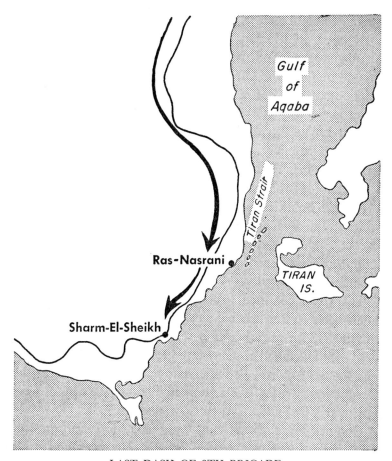

LAST DASH OF 9TH BRIGADE

By now the two landing craft were again steaming south on Aqaba Gulf bringing two AMX tanks from Elat. They arrived too late for the finish.

At 0900 on Monday, 5 November, just one week after Sharon marched, Yoffe was able to radio Dayan: "It is finished. Praised be God, the Creator of the Earth."

The maneuver out of which came the knockout blow had taken about five hours from the jump-off until the last shot was fired. The Egyptian main body was entrenched along a ridge crest running parallel to the coast with its right flank next to the sea. Though Israel's Air Force had strafed Sharm-El-Sheikh for two days, it had not damaged this position.

At 0400 hours six Israeli companies loaded into half-tracks which formed in line and started up the ridge. While the dark still held, they closed to within 150 yards of the defenders. At dawn several Israeli jets napalmed the trench line and the infantry then rushed it.

There was confused fighting in the trenches until three hours after sunrise when Lieut. Col. Khana Neguib at last surrendered his garrison. He had lost approximately two hundred men killed and as many wounded. He yielded more than one thousand able-bodied men who had been subdued in the direct assault by half their number. The brigade's losses were ten men killed and thirty-three wounded.

One of Yoffe's officers sought the senior Egyptian present, a full colonel who commanded the area. He was found at his bunker, dressed as for a parade. His bags were already packed and loaded onto a jeep, as was his batman. He had spent the battle hour preparing for his ride into captivity.

In its combat portions there is little that is either startling or instructive about this campaign. The chief merits of the Yoffe expedition are those which attend any human enterprise in which imaginative leadership inspires a following to believe that its collected power is invincible. The resolute will made possible the way.

Having attained the unattainable en route, the brigade had already won before coming under enemy fire. Its feat was memorable because of values which transcend anything pertaining to weapons and the men who bear them. Emphasized above all is the firepower in the human spirit when it is both daringly exploited and intelligently conserved. To push men to the limit—but to understand the limit—in this lies the touchstone of success in the fighting life or any other.

Men of the brigade got only thirty hours' rest beside the sea after the conquest of South Sinai. Then word came from the High Command that they were to hit the road for home. The return journey would be made via the Sinai west coast, where there are relatively decent roads. As an experiment, one detachment tried to return over the same route the brigade had come. It quickly found the way impassable and had to backtrack.

Yoffe's soldiers were not chagrined at the briefness of the respite. At heart they were farmers. It was the season. They knew they were needed for sowing the fields around Haifa.

So they cranked up and in eleven days after they had first formed up in soldier suits, they were home again, demobilized and working their farms. Within that interval, the brigade had traveled more than fourteen hundred miles under its own power.

Save for its battle losses, the brigade returned whole of mind and body. One man had collapsed, though whether from fear or dehydration, or the two working together, the doctors could not be certain. That was the only nonbattle casualty. There had been no illness and not one case of accident.

By comparison, the record shines for one more reason. During the attack into East Germany in the spring of 1945, the

United States Army went five hundred miles in thirty days. Unprecedented, the pace might have been still faster had there been less concern that the American front-line fighter might feel abused unless he was supplied with fresh eggs and oranges daily.

Still, everyone marveled that men and motors could endure the strain, and there was confident prediction among the warriors and logisticians that the marathon mark would long stand.

It did, until beaten by a brigade of Israeli farmers, with no claim to expertness in first-line maintenance, riding chariots of yesterday's design. Today they probably till their fields unaware that they hold a world's championship of sorts.

On this quiet note—the undemonstrative return of an army of fighting civilians to unheroic tasks much closer to their hearts—ended the campaign almost without parallel in its swift mobilization and application of energized courage.

Hugo Stophe, trap drummer in the orchestra of a Tel Aviv cocktail bar, was representative of many others. One night in October he quietly vanished and was gone six days. On the seventh night he was back beating his drums. Meanwhile he had fought a war. It had not changed life for Hugo; his mind was still on rhythm.

So it was with Israel. Clemenceau's phrase "the grandeur and misery of victory" did not apply to this singular people in the hour when their Army triumphed in Sinai. With few exceptions, life flowed normally and citizens went their accustomed rounds. They were too busy with their private enterprises to become beset by anxieties, doubts or the spirit of exultation.

They knew that their Army had performed miracles, but their almost casual reaction was as if they had expected nothing less, because the Army was of their own flesh and spirit. One of the by-products of pioneer-period fortitude is supposed to be a unifying calm amid general danger. During the hours of the great venture the self-possession of this people must have impressed all who beheld it.

From Dan to Beersheba, it was recognized that grave mistakes had been made during the world crisis. But in Israel, the people did not regard the thrust into Sinai and destruction of the Egyptian bases there as one of them. Emotionally, they were as well adjusted to the tide of military success as to the riptide of diplomatic frustration which followed. Expecting nothing to come easy, they rode above the storms of disappointment.

No mad flag-waving hailed the Sinai victory or was permitted to fan public excitement during the Sinai occupation. Hardly more than one score of Israel's fighting men were ever decorated for bravery on the field of battle, and these were mainly from the lower ranks. Whereby the various brigade and battalion commanders distinguished themselves through audacious decision and extraordinary personal initiative, the nation is still largely unaware. Very little was given the press on this subject. With exemplary modesty, the Army prefers not to make public heroes of its main personalities.

The imprint of several of them is inescapable. There lives quietly in Jerusalem a retired general, now giving his working time to archaeology. Yigael Yadin is still a relatively young man, with great personal charm and a mind which like a fine diamond reflects brilliant light from every facet. It was Yadin who, as chief of Israel's forces, had the faith to believe that the fate of a nation, even in our day, may be more safely entrusted to a citizen army than confided to a professional machine.

Where the scientist from Jerusalem left off, the farmer from Nahalal picked up. Moshe Dayan impresses those who

view him from afar as a highly romantic figure, in part because of his taut look and his black eyepatch, which he
would change for something less conspicuous if the surgeons
could work it out. In truth, there is nothing high tension or
self-assuming about him. He is the natural man, utterly without side, forthright in speech and in his personal manner, almost a homespun character.

While he led Israel's armed forces, it was almost impossible
to divert him conversationally from military problems and
theory. Now that he has a different interest, it will be given
the same single-minded attention.

The Sinai campaign was Dayan's masterpiece. Providing the
best measure of his genius as a soldier, it still says too little
directly about the command personality which by its radiance
energized a fighting system.

His subordinates speak first of his sparkling wit, which often
turns into a biting tongue. They comment on his brilliant
reasoning, his grasp of small tactics as well as broad strategy,
his ability to estimate the enemy correctly and his absolute
disdain for anyone on a staff not dedicated to the front-line
soldier. What seems to impress them even more is the grasp
which enables him to single out the essential problem, concentrate on it until he has reached the solution and then
implement it with a vigor which borders on ruthlessness.

He is not without idiosyncrasies. He has been known to
disparage an officer in front of his peers with words which
seemed to blast his career, only later to take a second reading
and treat him with high favor. In meetings of the Army Staff,
he has been known to take a decision after a showing of hands
which expressed the majority opinion. Capable of that when
he has no strong view of his own, he would just as readily
dictate a course when convinced of its soundness, though all
others are in opposition.

Thoroughly at home among soldiers and capable of putting fire into them on any occasion, Dayan is awkward in his press relationships, little skilled as a public speaker and inclined ever to limit the flow of useful information because of an excessively cautious view about security matters.

He ignores a physical handicap that would have ended the command career of a less determined man. Because of his eye injury, he is subject to frequent blinding headaches.

The most eloquent tribute which the General Staff in Israel continues to pay him, though he is no longer its chief, is when a member uses the simple phrase, "Moshe did *that* for us."

In the context of the conversation, the "that" refers mainly to the fact that Dayan made Israel's Army—reservists and professionals alike—mirror himself. Dayan as a fighting man holds to the conviction that in battle boldness usually pays off. The spontaneous unity when under fire of the men who form the brigades hardens out of this controlling idea.

While the Sinai campaign lasted, nothing else made possible the command resolution which held ranks to an almost excessively demanding line of duty. So it has ever been. There is little virtue in combat leadership except as the masterminding of tasks is based upon accurate, applied knowledge of the physical and spiritual limits and resources of the men who must fire the rifles, jockey the half-tracks, get the caissons rolling or, for that matter, man the Nike battery.

This fundamental truth, as it bears upon the complex task of getting the best possible performance from men in their hour of greatest danger, is best expressed in what was written almost half a century ago by John Masefield. He said:

The efforts of men are limited by their strength. The strength of men, always easily exhausted, is the only strength at the disposal of a general. It is the money to be spent by him in the purchase of victory, whether by hours of marching in the mud, digging in the field, or in attack. Losses in attack are great, though occasional. Losses from other causes are great and constant.

There could hardly be a more dire loss to national strength than occurs when generalship itself rejects the main lesson, neglecting the resources of the human spirit because of the hope that they flourish almost unattended and the illusion that the foundation of decisive power is formed of superior matériel.

Exalting super-weapons, the new age promotes that danger. Such is its strident tone and such the endless quest after greater technological sensations that one watching it in detachment might well believe that man himself, his ability to endure, his readiness when trained to match courage with courage, no longer weights the balance in human affairs.

Maybe it is only in this frame that the story of a last, small and rather old-style war would be found worth the reading. When the lamps are trimmed a little, we may return somewhat closer to the heart of things.

Appendix I...Notes on Training

STANDARDS

Israel's Army believes that it takes a minimum of thirty months' hard training to make a fit combat soldier. Every reservist has that much steady service behind him before qualifying for stand-by duty in a home-town unit. Both in the reserve and in the active Army, training is more rigorous, puts heavier emphasis on field combat exercises and makes heavier demand on the physical powers of the individual than in the United States Army.

There is no minimum educational requirement for induction. There is none for promotion or for elevation to, and within, the officer corps. All officers are made from the ranks. The average field-grade officer has less than a twelfth-grade education.

There is a minimum intelligence requirement for retention in the Army once the man is inducted. Every recruit must pass a basic examination designed to test his common sense, reasoning power and reaction time.

During training, the soldier is thrown more on his own than under the United States system. All instruction is pointed toward sharpening the power of decision in the average individual. Physical exercise and lecture courses are aimed to test and increase personal initiative. Israel's trainers believe that teaching the man to think clearly, observe keenly and report accurately is the main object in the school of the soldier.

Accordingly, relatively little importance is attached to perfection in the manual of arms, parade-ground drill and other routines familiar in Western armies.

MARCHES AND EXERCISES

Troops are kept moving about in open country as much as possible. The average recruit is strong in the legs, having hiked around since childhood. From the hour of his entry into service, he needs that muscle power, for it is pushed hard.

The Army wastes no time in road marching, believing that a thirty-mile movement across ridges does more to condition troops than seventy miles on the flat. Most marches are an approach to a combat exercise. Even when the reserves take their periodic training, they are kept in the open and are put over rough ground, traveling by night. Every camp is an armed bivouac on a position suitable for defense; no time is spent at a training base. Say the trainers: "That would be a waste. The men would be put on police tasks; we don't call that training." While in uniform, the reservists live away from their families, as would soldiers fighting a campaign, and they seem to like it better that way.

During training, the reservist subsists on hard field rations. No blankets or overcoats are issued for the bivouacs. The staff feels that the toughening process is furthered by letting the man sleep cold on the ground.

What the Army requires physically of its troops is illustrated in the testing course given the recruit, after it is decided that he is potential NCO material. Such aspirants are divided into packets of three; then each member of the team is put under a twenty-pound load, including his rifle and ammunition. Next, the team is given a march schedule which keeps it moving forty miles per day for three days running, through sharp ridges, such as are found in the Galilee country. Two thirds of the route is covered by day, the other by night, the whole taking approximately thirty hours of the three days.

In another test, the body of NCO candidates must march forty miles and finish in eight and one-half hours. No starter is permitted to fall out. If he shows signs of faltering, his comrades must help him along. If he fails, they must carry him.

The obstacle course, which tests the same class, is taken under pack and rifle. There is first a 400-meter run, which includes the scaling of a six-foot wall and the walking of a twenty-foot parallel bar. In the next 400-meter lap, the recruit must crawl on his belly fifteen yards under barbed wire, go through three ditches filled with running water, walk the plank over a fourth ditch ten-feet deep and throw a live grenade at a target. He then runs another six hundred yards free of obstacles. Provided he finishes the 1400-yard course in less than eleven minutes, he qualifies for a "silver rating."

NIGHT TRAINING

Though a night-fighting body, Israel's Army does not put preponderant emphasis on night training in its schedules. Rather, it follows the principle that programs of night and day training should be balanced according to a reasoned estimate of what will be required of a particular facility, or tactic, during combat.

As things work out, about one third of all training is done at night, including specialist training. But if, for example, it were estimated that 95 percent of all mine-laying would be done during the daylight, mine-laying would get little attention in night-training schedules.

Upon entering the Army, the inductee must serve at least six months as a private. But he may be tabbed for leadership immediately because of his personal qualities and a high IQ showing. In that event, he is sent quickly to section-leaders school, where he spends five months learning to handle what Americans call a squad.

Every week he works 52 hours or more. At first, he listens and obeys rather than attempts any leading. His instruction in the use of small arms will be divided, 12 hours by day, 4 by night. On terrain study, the use and making of maps and how to take up ground, he will spend 54 hours by day and 30 by night. On how to direct and control eight men during combat, he will get 22 hours of practice by day and 8 by night. All of this will be field work, away from the desk.

At the stage when he takes over and begins directing the squad (section) in its exercises, the work equation is as follows:

Ambush operations—12 hours' day, 11 night.
Attack on a village—5 hours' day, 3 night.
Squad in the general attack—34 hours' day, 12 night.

The totals are 103 hours' day training and 51 hours' night training. Beyond that, he gets 181 hours of lecturing on how to lead a section, which includes 10 hours on the principles of war and 12 hours around a sand table. Then he spends another 98 daytime hours and 64 nighttime hours in exercises where his section operates within a platoon. At the end he is qualified to be a corporal and is posted to a unit, either to lead a section or to become an instructor.

As a basic soldier, he is paid ten dollars per month, with no allowance to his family. The reservist is paid the same, but gets compensation for his family from both government and his employer, which brings his total income to eighty percent of civilian pay.

CADET NIGHT TRAINING

After being made an NCO, the soldier must work at noncomship for at least six months even if he is unmistakably officer material. If he has the quality, he can go before the officer selection board, provided he first signs a contract to serve as an officer for at least one year.

Israel commissions about eight hundred men annually, of whom approximately three hundred enter infantry service. The same school trains officers for the combat arms and the technical services; the tech officers are given an extra polishing later. The age for conscription is eighteen. The average age of the newly commissioned second lieutenant in the standing army of Israel is nineteen; in the reserve, twenty-three. A company commander's average age is twenty-three; battalion commander, thirty-two.

The basic course for officership lasts six months. One sixth of the time is devoted to practice as a support-fire officer. During the cadet's training, he spends 341 hours in daytime combat exercises and 124 hours at night.

The classes are sent for a week at a time into mountain country, where they practice patrol leading, approach marching and leadership of the platoon in the attack. They march twenty-five to thirty miles each night and get their rest (except for debriefing practice) during the day.

In minor tactics, the time is divided about as follows:

Raiding—14 hours' day, 12 night.
Ambushing—10 hours' day, 2 night.
Patrolling—16 hours' day, 68 night.

In exercises devoted to the platoon in the attack, the division of training time is 55 daylight hours, 18 at night. The platoon in general defense takes 64 day hours and 6 night hours, one third of which is given to preparation of the night position.

CONSERVATION

All training programs, including the first instruction given the recruit, stress the conservation of human energy during combat and the danger of overextending operations by assigning tasks which are not within the physical limits of men.

"Never overload the soldier; rest him whenever possible." Reiterated at all stages of training, the two rules become ingrained in the junior leader. Says the Staff: "We learned the hard way that this is the road to salvation."

During training, one third of body weight is the maximum load permitted the soldier. That includes uniform, pack and all else. During combat, the load is lightened, according to the theory that his energy will be less under fire, rather than more.

Training exercises are kept "realistic." This is to say that a platoon or battalion in the simulated attack is not required to make a longer approach march than it could well do, were fire present, without pushing itself to exhaustion.

"Don't be too eager; don't pile on the pressure," has an odd sound, coming from a General Staff. It's said in Israel to junior leaders by way of emphasizing that men should be rested at every opportunity, instead of settling on them that extra fatigue during the mounting-up process which comes from needless anxiety in the command chain.

Elsewhere, it's a too familiar story. The colonel says, "Be ready at 0900." So the captain tells his platoon leaders, "Be ready at 0800," and they tell the section leaders, "Be ready at 0700."

Israel's Army shuns this practice like a plague. The recruit, on his way to become an NCO, is told that if he checks his men, and they look relatively ready, even though they are still sleeping, it's a sign of weakness in him if he routs them out ten minutes too early merely to further his own peace of mind.

SHARPSHOOTING

There are eight snipers in each infantry battalion and the Army values them as "worth their weight in gold." They are trained to take up ground individually, working well ahead or to the flank of the company in the attack. They become expert in scouting, map reading, the interpretation of front-line intelligence and use of the rifle. The sniperscope is carried in the pocket and slips onto the weapon in one click.

Recently the General Staff has looked at a new problem: "How do we get *aimed* fire at night?" It is seeking the answer in an original system of muscle and eye co-ordination and is confident that the results are justifying the experiment. Under training conditions, according to the Staff, with this new method the average Israeli rifleman can be fairly sure of hitting a kneeling man at night three times out of four at seventy-five yards' range. The theory and method have not been proved in combat. But the Staff believes that the solution lies in sharpening the senses of the rifleman rather than in the use of infrared scopes or other special equipment.

SQUAD ORGANIZATION

Israel Army is built up around an eight-man infantry section, the leader of which carries a submachine gun as does one other man. There are also two light machine guns within the section and four riflemen, one of whom is a specialist antitank grenadier.

In its attack formation during daylight, the section moves with the leader, the grenadier and one machine gunner forward as a three-man point. The others are deployed some paces to the rearward, two men on one flank, three on the other, so that the formation looks about like this:

In the night attack the formation stays the same in front, but the five other men trail behind it in column. If it is necessary for one man to scout the country two hundred yards or so in front of the section, the leader takes the assignment, armed with his submachine gun. Platoon and company commanders abide by the same rule in a similar situation. At battalion level and above, it is not done.

By Israeli training practice, when the light machine guns are used as a fire base to cover the forward movement of the rest of the section, they should not operate at more than two hundred yards' maximum range from the target. To cut that distance by half is considered better. In the attack LMG's are rated as highly expendable items and are shoved far front. When the section rushes the enemy position under cover of the LMG fire, one rifleman stays back to protect the gunners. It looks like this:

Israel's infantry prefers the rifle-fired antitank grenade to the bazooka for shock effect on a group or bunker. At night, if the section should run into an ambush, the grenadier fires and all the others rush straight in, not firing.

Rifle and LMG ammunition are interchangeable. There are sixty magazines carried within the squad, twenty bullets to a clip, or twelve hundred rounds altogether. Each submachine gunner carries 125 rounds. Within the squad are fourteen grenades, eight defensive, four offensive and two smoke.

WOMEN IN SERVICE

In Israel's Army there is a higher proportion of women in service than in the United States Army. Eligible, physically able young women are drafted, though there are exemptions because of religious scruples, married status, etc. After entering upon training, they are employed according to their talents. In contrast to what is done in the United States' services, they are fitted into the lower combat echelons, as signalers, clerks, etc., when they are emotionally disposed toward this kind of work even though it is attended by danger. Their presence in the zone of fire is believed to have an uplifting influence on the morale of the fighting force. Even the male fighters so say.

The literature, radio and other conditioning influences in Israel put less accent on glamour and sex than is the case in the United States. The Army's problem is eased proportionately. Soldiers say, "We get along better because there are more women around than in other armies." But that doesn't half explain it. The association between men and women in service is marked by a mutually supporting comradeship, high respect for the dignity of every other person and a common decency. The males act neither protectively nor superciliously toward the females. In the field, the attitude is as natural and relaxed as if they were together in a college classroom.

Women soldiers assigned to combat units are trained in the use of weapons. That is a safeguard rather than a key to their employment during fighting operations; they are used in the field on support tasks such as radio operator, supply clerk or cryptographer. A few women soldiers have qualified as paratroopers mainly because the General Staff couldn't resist the pressure to grant them this measure of equality. However, no woman soldier was parachuted into Sinai.

During the Sinai occupation the "Charms" were used in all kinds of security missions interchangeably with the male soldier. The nickname comes naturally. The Hebrew name for Woman's Army is "Hayl Nashim." When pronounced, the Hebrew initial letters of the corps mean "charm." This word picture of one such soldier doing duty was written early in the occupation:

You may go any day to the market place in Gaza. Some hundreds of Palestinian Arabs will be milling around, buying and selling. The market crowd is composed almost exclusively of adult males, Arab youths and children. Moving through it, free as air, and altogether unattended, goes one Israeli Charm, age nineteen. She carries a Tommy gun rather loosely over her shoulder. Any male in the crowd might wrest it from her before she could bring the weapon to bear.

But of that danger, she seems totally unaware. She goes her way laughing, as if hugely enjoying her day as a one-woman patrol. And oddly enough, the crowd appears to react to her as naturally as if she had always been there. No glares follow her. She is greeted as she passes. She is not shouldered, but on the other hand, no one jumps deferentially from her path.

WOMAN'S ARMY TRAINING

In the Woman's Army of Israel, there has never been a case of hysteria or loss of emotional control when under machine-gun fire or artillery bombardment.

The candidates for military service are given a psychological screening six months prior to induction to determine emotional fitness and aptitude. The tests became standardized in 1950 and the work has been carried out since at the mobilization depots. Irrespective of I.Q. or educational background, if anything in the candidate's personality or history indicates that she is emotionally unstable, she is rejected at the time of the screening.

Women soldiers serve two years, and save for officers, they are all in the 18–20 age group. If an Israeli girl marries before that age, she is still drafted, required to take basic training, and then put in a reserve unit.

Recent arrivals in Israel may be inducted into military service up to age 26 if still unmarried.

A girl of 17 may enlist voluntarily if she has just finished high school and prefers to fulfill her military obligation before going on to other things.

Should a girl be in college when she comes of draft age, she is permitted to get her degree before serving.

The pre-induction screening determines which potential draftees are qualified to become non-commissioned officers, specialists, file closers, etc. On being drafted, the woman soldier is already tabbed for the role in which she will best serve the army, and after basic training, her course is regulated accordingly.

What work the girl has done in civil life bears only indirectly on the MOS (military occupational specialty) that she is given by the Army. It is a controlling principle that the Army should broaden her horizons rather than hold her to duties which she may have never liked. For example, if the girl has done menial chores, such as those of a housemaid or scrubwoman, it is a rigid rule that she will not be put on menial work while in uniform. She is likely to be detailed to

Nakhl, the reforestation organization where she can live in the open.

The creator and chief of the Woman's Army since its beginnings soon after the birth of the nation is Col. Shoshana Gershom, a comely woman whose charm gets no less while the years get more. She had long service with the British Army in Italy during World War II. Superficially her training and administrative system is modeled on the British pattern, but the controlling ideas and philosophy are native to Israel.

Of the personnel policy, Col. Gershom says: "I would take it for granted that any woman who disliked her civilian work would feel doubly degraded if the Army held her to the same task. It is not normal in a woman to love military service in any case. So we try to assign duties which will make the soldier feel uplifted."

Col. Gershom has other novel ideas. She believes that women in uniform must look neater and be militarily more exacting than males if they are to play their parts effectively. Her main disciplinary problem comes of the fact that the girls hate military hats and carry them under their arms.

Cases of scandalous misconduct or sex misbehavior are rare in the Woman's Army. Where reform is clearly impossible, Col. Gershom has authority to discharge any woman soldier within twenty-four hours. If the psychiatrists feel that the case is not hopeless, the rule followed is that the Army provides the best environment for reform.

If the woman soldier commits a military offense, she may be charged by any officer of the Army. But only a female officer may try or disqualify her.

For women soldiers, the basic training-period is six weeks. Approximately one-third of that time is given to the school of the soldier, with emphasis on the care, handling and firing of weapons, including the rifle, sten gun and grenade. They are also schooled in field maintenance and the tactical employment of ground. But there is no squad drill.

After basic training, there follows specialist schooling, the average course taking about six weeks. If the girl is marked to become an NCO, she goes two and one-half months to NCO school.

Following training, the soldier is then assigned to a field unit. Practically the whole of Woman's Army is operational and functionally auxiliary to the Army as a whole, almost no strength being wasted on interior administration.

Col. Gershom's GHQ group and personal staff comprises just seven individuals, including her Deputy, driver and several clerks.

The whole training inflow feeds through but two training companies, each with a maximum strength of 400. Save for this establishment, no Israeli unit is composed exclusively of women soldiers.

For each 100 women in training, there are but one woman officer and one woman sergeant to direct the training activities. Only women instructors are assigned, though males are called on for lectures.

Women soldiers are used as outguards and patrols in the protection of the frontier settlements; so they need to know how weapons work though they are not regarded as "fighters."

They fit into other such tasks as cryptographer, steno typist, radio or radar operator, motor mechanic, driver, parachute rigger and first-aid specialist. Women soldiers are not used as cooks and KP's but they may be made mess sergeants in administrative charge of the feeding and dining arrangements of troops, if their talents so qualify them.

During peacetime, however, the commanding task of the Woman's Army is teaching. Many illiterate males, recently arrived in Israel, are drafted into the Army. They cannot talk

Hebrew, much less read and write it. This handicap perforce makes them second-class citizens in the social sense at least.

It is the task of the Charms to provide the teaching which makes them literate by the time they are discharged by the Army.

Some slight friction comes of that. The adult male Israeli soldier instinctively resents taking elementary instruction from a girl in uniform. The teaching is according to standards set by the Ministry of Culture. Along with the woman soldier, it regards the male attitude as just another hairshirt which has to be worn.

Only fourteen members of the Woman's Army have taken jump training and qualified as paratroopers.

"I was opposed to it," said Col. Gershom, "and so were the males on the General Staff. But when people are ambitious, they need to be humored."

The woman soldier stays in the reserve until she becomes thirty-four unless motherhood has intervened; even then, she may still volunteer to continue the obligation.

INDOCTRINATION

Once a month, the Education Department of the Army's GHQ publishes a pamphlet about the land, its social problems, political goals, etc., for the benefit of troops.

The information is the précis for an orientation lecture. Each unit commander is supposed to give such a talk to his troops at monthly intervals. Like the average American officer, he dislikes the chore, tries to brush it off and sometimes succeeds.

Though Israel is a new nation and a melting of peoples with many tongues coming from everywhere, the Army attaches relatively little importance to the proposition that training for better citizenship, and clearer understanding by the soldier of his cause, is the one best way to build military unity and stimulate the fighting spirit.

The General Staff regards indoctrination as one more means of habituating officers to stand before their own people and talk—the chief value deriving from the program. The General Staff spokesman said, "It is our contract to take an average civilian and make of him an efficient, successful fighting man, skilled at arms and proud of his unit because it has combat power; we believe that out of his Army experience, he will almost automatically mature into full, co-operative citizenship."

DOCTRINE AND DECISION

Toward heightening the power of decision in all ranks, the Army's doctrine as published by High Command, or expressed by a section leader, emphasizes task, mission, objective above everything else.

"The battle will never go as you planned it; but you still have your task," epitomizes the main idea. Along with positiveness of aim, there is proportionate emphasis accordingly on flexibility of means. When given a mission, the leader is told that he will exercise his own judgment about how to perform the task if his instructions prove unsuitable. But he cannot withdraw without permission.

Such phrases as "at all costs" are avoided in Army orders because of their ambiguity. The patrol sent to reconnoiter with instructions to avoid detection may return at will if sighted by the enemy. On the other hand, a patrol of the same size, if sent to destroy a roadblock, must stay with the task as long as any chance remains that it can be accomplished.

The patrol can't quit simply because it has been badly shot up. But if in the judgment of the leader, it has taken so many casualties that the able-bodied have been immobilized by the weight of the wounded, he may withdraw without permission, and his decision will be accepted if the facts prove consistent with the Army's rigorous standard.

The radical disregard of supply sufficiency which marked Army operations in the Sinai campaign directly reflects teaching by the Army trainers. Leaders are told: "Logistical means are of secondary importance. Things are never perfect. It's more risky to wait. So go on and hit. Don't drag your feet because supply is short. The means will come to you. You've got to take a chance."

One brigade commander expressed the doctrine this way: "In combat I plan my move. Briefly I go over it with my staff to sharpen their appreciation of the next action. If I learn that ammunition and fuel supply are less than that minimum which would certainly enable me to close on the enemy position, I reconsider. Then if the essential supply is less than 50 percent of what I think I need, I would think twice before moving, and would feel justified in postponing action. But if supply is half or more of my estimated need, I would attack, unless the reading of the situation convinced me I had no chance whatever."

Another said: "The principle holds all down the line that each level has discretionary power and nothing is absolutely rigid. But we of the line have a right to demand of the logistical system that it keep up. Why not? It's geared to the same pace we are. If I let fears about it dictate my moves in combat, that would lessen the pressure on it to stay abreast of me. The result would be watered-down decisions from front to rear."

IN COMBINATION

Where the combined arms move together on the battlefield, the governing principle is that continuity in integration and in general assignment of task is the best insurance of performance.

Relationships between armor and infantry, hitting as a team, remain flexible; where command is placed depends on the nature of the tactical task, the ground and the personalities of the several commanders. The one guiding rule is to avoid change, according to the observation that every reintegration of forces during combat diminishes hitting power.

As much as possible, infantry is directed to attack by night, thereby to further both surprise and protection, since darkness is a form of cover. Where there is no choice but to attack by day, infantry is supposed to move with close support by armor, though not using it as a shield. The infantry should be within five minutes' closing distance of the enemy line when the preliminary air strike comes in so that it can grapple before the shock is gone. Except that it puts less accent on field-artillery support, this part of the Army's doctrine has a familiar pattern.

SOMETHING NEW ADDED

During the Sinai fighting, the General Staff concluded that reserve officers have less capacity than "regulars" for a quick shift of direction amid battle and the making of a bold decision.

The civilian leader undeviatingly responded to orders. He was less apt to see the opening clearly and change his line abruptly when the battle became fluid. That was understandable; thirty days' training per year provides too little exercise in "adaptability."

So something new was tried to test and make more acute the decision-making faculty in reservists. It is a three-day command-post exercise which starts at a slow trot and finishes like a cavalry charge.

The battalion commander is taken into the field with his staff, communications people, his company commanders and their operations network. Then he is given a tactical exercise

out of a variety—capture of a tank-defended town, attack on a
fortified ridge, breakthrough of a fortified pass, destruction of
a major roadblock, etc.

On the first day, all of his means for careful calculation of
decision are present. He is given twenty-two hours to form a
plan. Air photos and maps are available. Any amount of
reconnaissance is permitted, as is unlimited consultation with
his staff, though all hands must act as if they are in the presence of the enemy. He commands through written orders.
Control officers are down with his company commanders and
they feed back information about how the situation is developing. In the end, he delivers his plan and movement order
to the brigade.

At that moment, he's told, "Everything's changed. Your
H-Hour remains the same. But the brigade is making a ninety-
degree change in direction. It's been stopped on the right. So
that's your target—that hill over there. There's no time for
reconnaissance. Here are the maps and air photos. You'll have
to move in thirty minutes. We want your decision before
then."

In the interval, the control officers are shoving information
to the companies and it comes back to battalion in full flow
while the chief and his staff are weighing what to do. The
pressure builds up, up, toward the climax.

The worst bump comes as the battalion commander pre-
sents his second plan. He is told, "Again, everything's changed.
The enemy is cracking on the right. You've lost half your force.
You attack straight ahead against Hill 300. There's no time for
map checking or staff talk. We want your decision right now."

In the final phase, the statement of enemy strength and the
distance to be traveled makes sound solution of the problem
barely within his limits of time and men. It remains just possible to take the objective. The commander's decision therefore initiates a workable plan only if, in his mind, speed of

thought presages rapidity of movement and daring improvisation. The primary idea is to sharpen faculties; the secondary
idea is to test their sufficiency under emergency conditions.

Every battalion commander is put through this mill. Change
in the character of the exercise is constant. Some of the prepa-
rations have general application. But it is left to the brigade
commanders to write the exercises according to what patterns
they judge will provide the most practical and decisive tests.
GHQ reviews the plan and makes the controlled stores and
umpire personnel available.

Some battalion commanders, given this processing, become
completely shocked. Others meet its challenge without turning
a hair. Along the road, higher command learns which officers
excel at planning, which at on-the-spot improvisation and
which at control. As personal weaknesses become revealed,
further training is directed toward producing balanced "adaptability."

BALANCE OF FORCES

Another lesson drawn from the Sinai campaign by the General Staff is that the reserve is almost unmanageably top-heavy
in logistical units, whereas the standing Army is dispropor-
tionately strong in fighting power with too little motor means
either for rapid self-movement or for servicing reserve concentration and deployment once mobilization starts.

Reserve trains and other supply units must be converted
into infantry, and some of the standing Army's combat parts
must be changed into line-of-supply units to afford a better
balance. The shift is an expensive and time-consuming process.

RESERVE CUTBACK

In Israel, force levels are not set by law. There is no such
problem as the Army having to fight for its existence; very few
members of the Knesset are actively antimilitary. The armed

establishment is given a lump sum appropriation according to the availability of money. It is then up to the General Staff to write the equation—how much can be spent on reserve training, what size standing force can be supported, what must be apportioned to procurement, etc. The Army figures that it costs five times as much to maintain a professional soldier as to train a conscript. Hence the continuing tendency is to narrow the standing force while broadening and strengthening the reserve manpower base.

Due to the high cost of the Sinai campaign, however, and the need for structural reforms indicated by the mobilization, that aim is being temporarily diverted. The funds won't stretch far enough to pay for conversion and still maintain old standards. Israel's Army has about decided that the most practical economy is to slash reserve training.

Here is another risk-filled decision. Readiness in its civilian soldiery has been the rock of Israel's security since the reserve was first formed and given its character in the design drawn by the inspired soldier-scientist, Gen. Yigael Yadin. His hand made the body even as General Dayan's philosophy about boldness in combat decision and concentration on task breathed into it a new and dynamic spirit.

Israel's law prescribes that a reservist shall not be given more than thirty days' continuous training per year and one day refresher training per month. That legal limit doubles the training stint of the average U.S. National Guardsman. But it's merely the statement of an ideal standard.

Prior to Sinai, the average civilian soldier in Israel got not more than two weeks' training annually. The look of greater combat readiness in its reserve is hence not to be found in length of training time but in the stern use made of it.

Under the new economy, the Army proposes to limit reserve training to officers and NCO's, down to section leader.

It reasons, perhaps from necessity, that training money spent on part-time private soldiers is largely wasted because they forget too easily.

Reserve battalions will be called up separately twice yearly for three-day training intervals. Men and officers will get one day's schooling in weapons handling to quicken their technical knowledge. After that, the formation will go into a tactical exercise, such as the attack on a fortified position.

The brigade commander will be present with his staff and communications net. He will direct the instruction and oversee the planning. Though only one battalion will be present for maneuver, the brigade exercise will otherwise be conducted full-dress—with pyrotechnics, bangalores and live ammunition in the supporting weapons. In a first go at this kind of thing, several of the participants were wounded. Staff observers marked the experiment "successful."

Apart from the abbreviated battalion training, two or three brigades will be called up annually for two weeks of maneuvering, so that higher command may keep its hand practiced. Through the year, 50 percent of reserve unit commanders will be called to take brief courses in the staff schools. The other half will have to wait until the next year.

This contracted program, the Army hopes, will be sufficient to keep the command apparatus intact and healthy. It's far from the ideal. But it's the most that the nation can afford.

Appendix II...The Air Battle

LIMITATIONS

For the attacking Israeli Air Force, Sinai was an almost classic battleground because of the nakedness of the country, the clear definition of targets and the restrictions upon the enemy's movement overland.

To assist the land fighting, the air support had to watch the lines of three highways and one railroad, and nothing much more, since it had been forbidden to attack Egyptian bases in the Gaza Strip. That simplified interdictory operations. They proceeded on the theory that the dunes and desert rock would keep the Egyptian columns pretty much roadbound. This theory proved to be correct.

But there were offsetting restrictions. From the beginning, Israel's pilots were ordered to stay at least ten miles east of the Suez Canal. Not one pilot violated the order, the purpose of which, at the start, was to "keep the operation looking as small as possible."

Because of the order, Israel's Air Force remained on the defensive throughout. In the first days, it was hard doing. The Egyptian Air Force remained intact, its bases and fields untouched. Israeli pilots flying parallel with the line of the Canal could look westward and see part of this almost motionless array. Why didn't the enemy strike back?

The question was never answered. The first guess was that

Egypt's Air thought that Israel's opening maneuver was a limited effort, not worth going after. Later it was concluded that its pilots and other people lacked that degree of readiness which is requisite in modern air power.

MITLA COVER

At Mitla Pass Israel's Air Force dropped in broad daylight a parachute battalion thirty-five miles from the nearest Egyptian air base. The carriers moved under jet-fighter cover. Where the transport aircraft flew low, the jets flew at high altitude because of their greater fuel consumption. Egypt must have picked up the jet formations on radar one hundred miles before they got above the drop zone. Still, nothing happened.

Israel's Air realized that it was almost impossible for the carrier force to get perfect protection from the high-altitude cover. The solution was to put forward a fighter screen which flew north-to-south ten miles inside the Canal at varying heights. The screen cluttered up the enemy radar, permitted direct observation of the possible enemy take-off and promised to draw off the Egyptian fighters if they headed for Mitla Pass.

For a half-hour before the drop occurred, and for another half-hour following, the jets on this patrol flew the whole length of the Canal. From thirty thousand feet, the pilots could see the MiG's lined up on the Egyptian runways. They watched them being towed away into dispersal; but that was all. Said one pilot who made this patrol, "It was heartbreaking."

Israel anticipated that Sharon's Brigade would be interrupted by air attack on its night march to Nakhl. The brigade rode with all headlights on, the roughness of the country and tightness of the schedule making it necessary. Yet no air cover could be provided for it because of demands elsewhere. Again, the enemy Air Force did not react as expected.

ASSUMPTIONS

In its planning, Israel's Air Staff assumed that the Egyptians would attack Israel's air bases first and its cities next, or strike both types of targets together. So in the opening hours, extra risks had to be run by the ground columns; part of Israel's air strength stayed contained to go after Egypt's air bases.

The occasion did not arise. When on the first morning, Egyptian jets struck Sharon's column, Israel's Air Staff guessed that the anticipated main danger had passed. The four Vampires which attacked Sharon were taken on by two Mystères after they had made their last pass. All four were shot down on the way home. It wasn't a fight but a chase.

Up till that point, Israel's Air Force had operated as cover and nothing else. Immediately thereafter, it sought and received permission from the High Command to go after the enemy ground forces in Sinai. There was one slight reservation: a string had to be kept on part of the Air Command so that if the calculation about Egyptian inertia proved wrong, there could be swift retaliation against the nearest enemy bases. The Air Staff interpreted this decision with an elasticity that took care of everything, irrespective of the plane count. The Air Force would hit enemy ground forces wherever they appeared in the open. When the brigades called for a preliminary strike or other direct support mission, it would be flown. Whatever was left would be the counter-punch force ready to swing on the body of Egypt.

The green light switched on at noon that same day. Two reports came in together, one that an enemy column had crossed the Canal and was headed toward Abu Agueila, the other that out of Suez a convoy of trucks and tanks was speeding east toward Mitla Pass. Naturally, the southern column became the first target since Sharon's dropped battalion was highly exposed. In brewing-up the road column, Israel's jets flew three hundred miles from their own bases to within twenty miles of the Egyptian bases. Still, they were not taken on.

AIR AGAINST GROUND

There had as yet been no sign of Egyptian aircraft abandoning their bases. During the second night, Israel's Air Force had aircraft flying the three main east-west highways to observe and also to beat down enemy columns moving east from the Canal. The convoys came on with lights burning—splendid targets. About 120 trucks, tanks and troop carriers were caught on the road, rocketed and napalmed. Some of them escaped unhurt, dispersed amid the desert scenery and thereafter did not move during darkness. They were caught coming back onto the roads at dawn, the east-west patrolling having continued through the night.

ON D PLUS TWO

On Wednesday the Air Force undertook two main tasks, attacking along all main roads against enemy armor and transport in motion, and flying support to Sharon's Brigade when it bucked through the Mitla Pass. From Suez the Egyptian armor, with some accompanying infantry, made a half-hearted try to join this fight, got a few miles into Sinai and was smashed by air attack, jets and prop-driven craft being used.

This was the only day when the Egyptian Air Force accepted the challenge and there were numerous engagements, fighter against fighter. Most of them started in the zone twenty-five to thirty-five miles from the Canal where the Israeli planes were flying cover. Because the cover had to be continuous, Israel's Air Force could only put up a limited number of jets at one time. In consequence, in all eight engagements they were in the first stage outnumbered. The positions of the cover planes had to stay more or less fixed, where they would be on the Egyptian radarscope at all times.

As to tactics, the Egyptians handled MiG's about the way they were used in Korea, flying in staggered formations at various heights and trying to break off engagement by climbing turns. Their pilots seemed to dislike to tighten these turns and Israel's Air Force got the impression that their shooting was not very good.

In the dogfighting, Israel's Air Force shot down five MiG 15's, six Vampires and one Meteor. It lost one aircraft air-to-air—a Piper Cub shot down near Kuntilla. Another Piper was destroyed on the ground while serving Sharon's Brigade. Two Israeli jets were lost to ground fire.

After this day there were no enemy aircraft to be seen. For the Air Force, the rest of the war was interdiction and the flying of close support missions. Though that part sounds routine, it was more rugged than the air dueling. Israel's pilots do their strafing, with rockets and napalm, at twenty-five to thirty feet above ground level. The threat of napalm almost invariably aborted the Egyptian crews from their vehicles or bunkers before it hit. But it didn't dampen machine-gun and small-arms fire from along the edges of the strike. This was one thing that the enemy did very well—pouring in volume fire as the plane swept through. Several F-51's were knocked down by rifle bullets.

But napalm and rockets will not destroy hard-surfaced roads, and Israel had no bombs that would blast a wide, deep crater. The best that could be done was to create partial roadblocks by continuing to burn out convoys as far westward as possible. So the jets kept moving back to the deadline some miles east of Qantara, Ismailia and Suez.

HELP FOR YOFFE

In the hour when Egypt's Army in the north quit fighting, Israel's Air Force started operations over South Sinai. Sharm-El-Sheikh was strafed repeatedly before Yoffe's Brigade drew near it. That was how Israel lost one Mystère; it was knocked off by flak in attacking Ras-Nasrani. A 30 mm round scored a direct hit on the engine. The pilot bailed out and landed two miles from the Egyptian camp. Other jets came in to orbit around him and hold the enemy infantry off while a Piper was flown all the way from Elat to pick him up.

The air attack on Sharm-El-Sheikh continued two days. In midmorning of the third day, a pilot saw two ships approaching the port, one a frigate, the other a transport, loaded with troops. The troopship was sunk; the frigate got away, somewhat damaged. Thereby ended Egypt's one attempt to reinforce the last position.

The commander ashore, Lieutenant Colonel Neguib, said he lost his battle on the ground before Yoffe's Brigade got there. Two days of air strafing was more than he could stand; the rockets and napalm did him in. He said, "I learned about close air support during my schooling in England, or so I thought, until I stood at Sharm-El-Sheikh."

MAIN DECISION

By the Air Staff's reckoning, its main decision, in conflict with what is elsewhere considered the controlling principle, came when its forces were committed full-scale to support of the land battle without first achieving air superiority or inflicting any material damage on the enemy Air Force.

After the French and British intervened, first to bomb the Egyptian bases, then to land at Port Said, Israel's Air Force had no operational changes to make; its planes were already restricted to limits which kept them from the Suez zone. Israel's Air Force at no time had radio contact with the allied aviation; it knew of the latter's movements only as they were reported by the press services.

One British pilot bailed out five miles beyond Israel's lines near Qantara. An infantry patrol went forth in an attempt to rescue him. Four British jets orbited around the pilot and drove the patrol back with fire. This happened after all fighting was supposed to be stopped.

BACKGROUND

Israel trains all of its own pilots from the ground up though the opportunity stays open to send them abroad for technical courses. The High Command feels that the advantages of schooling the man on home ground far outweigh the value of the additional knowledge which might be picked up from other systems.

The main problem is the language. All operations are conducted in Hebrew, as is all teaching. The smallness of the vocabulary and the paucity of adverbs, adjectives and abstract nouns make Hebrew a difficult language to assist the growth of a steadily expanding technology. To meet the needs of the modern state, it has had to be amplified with word forms and sounds which are quite foreign. The Hebrew military dictionary as now used in Israel has grown even more rapidly than the Army. As medieval grammar demanded Arabic terms, so modern science requires European terms, though when these terms are fitted into the structure of Hebrew, they are almost inevitably corrupted. Israel's Air Staff believes that the technician's mastery of nomenclature, procedures, etc., in this period when the operational vocabulary is growing so rapidly, would undergo compound difficulty if he were trained elsewhere.

The Army has for the first time a truly sufficient reserve of pilots. Their tactical training emphasizes close support of infantry-armor above any other employment, and one of its premises is that an Air Force pilot must know terrain from the view of an infantry commander.

CO-OPERATION

In two instances during the Sinai campaign, Air Force fire was directed at its own ground forces. That was not due strictly to the swift changes of situation or the fact that the fire lines were so close joined. To further their own mobility the attacking columns began using Egyptian tanks and trucks, which are painted a conspicuous yellow, as rapidly as they were captured. Diffusing the target, it confused the pilots.

Appendix III...Outline and Chronology

Movement

A. Northern Axis: Rahfa—El Arish—Qantara
B. Central Axis: Nitzana—Abu Agueila—Ismailia
C. Southern Axis: Kuntilla—Nakhl—Suez
D. Eastern Axis: Ras-el-Nagb—Dahab—Sharm-El-Sheikh

Egyptian Bases

A. Gaza—governmental and administrative base
B. Khan Yunis—headquarters of 8th Infantry Division
C. Rahfa—logistical base
D. El Arish—main logistical base and headquarters of 3rd Infantry Division; air base
E. Abu Agueila—brigade base
F. Themed—main base for desert forces
G. Nakhl—training base of fedayeen forces
H. Sharm-El-Sheikh—main base for South Sinai and Gulf of Aqaba; air base
I. Bir Gifgafa—armored and air base
J. Bir Hamm—armored and air base

Egyptian Dispositions

A. Theater headquarters at Ismailia
B. 8th Infantry Division (three brigades) holding the Gaza Strip, Rahfa excluded
C. 3rd Infantry Division (three infantry brigades and one armored battalion) holding Rahfa, El Arish, Jebel Libni, Abu Agueila and Queisima

D. Two battalions of the Desert Patrol holding the Southern Axis
E. Two battalions holding the Sharm-El-Sheikh sector
F. Various administrative and supporting units serving the main bases and covering defiles and outpost positions

Egyptian Reserves

A. 2nd Infantry Division in the Canal Zone
B. One armored brigade in the Canal Zone
C. 1st Infantry Division and one armored division in Cairo and to its south

Israeli Field Army (with one exception, brigade numbers remain secret)

1ST TASK FORCE
Infantry Brigade "A" (Givli)
Armored Brigade "L" (Barlev)

2ND TASK FORCE
Infantry Brigade "B" (Harpaz)
Infantry Brigade "C"
Armored Brigade "M" (Ben-Ari)

UNDER GHQ
Airborne Brigade "X" (Sharon)
Infantry (motorized) Brigade "D" (the 9th under Yoffe)
Infantry Brigade "E" minus one rifle battalion, plus several companies of armor (Doron)

Chronology of the Campaign

1. *29 October 1956—D Day*
   Central Axis. After sunset Brigade "B" crosses the frontier, advancing toward Queisima.
   Southern Axis. At sunset Brigade "X," having crossed the frontier earlier that day, attacks Kuntilla, en route to Mitla Pass, where one of its paratroop battalions has been dropped in late afternoon.

2. *30 October—D plus 1.*

Central Axis. In early morning Brigade "B" captures Queisima. At noon Brigade "M" passes through Queisima. That afternoon one of its armored teams probes the Abu Agueila fortified ridges from the south and its reconnaissance company gets on the rear of the Abu Agueila position. Late in the day Brigade "B" sends a spearhead south to Nakhl to link with Brigade "X." After dark troops of Brigade "C" attack and capture positions on the road west of Nitzana.

Southern Axis. Brigade "X" captures the Themed position at dawn, and at sunset captures Nakhl. Through the day Egyptian forces attack the defensive circle of the paratroop battalion dropped east of Mitla Pass. The overland column of Brigade "X" joins the battalion shortly before midnight.

3. *31 October—D plus 2.*

Central Axis. One combat team of Brigade "M" captures Abu Agueila in early morning, blocks the roads from El Arish and Ismailia, and in late evening assaults and captures the nearest fortified ridge. The second combat team attacks westward and passes Jebel Libni. The third team attacks south and captures Bir Hasne. Brigade "C" attacks the Abu Agueila hedgehog from the east but is stopped.

Southern Axis. At noon a heavily reinforced battalion task force from Brigade "X" advances to reconnoiter Mitla Pass and becomes well trapped within a heavily fortified defile. The whole brigade is drawn into this action through the afternoon. The fight is broken off, then resumed after dark and successfully completed within two hours. With the capture of Mitla Pass by Brigade "X" Egyptian resistance along the Southern Axis ends.

Northern Axis. Preparatory to the general assault on the Rahfa position, after the sun goes down Brigade "A" begins to advance its forces up to and through the mine field barrier covering the frontier, which it had gapped the night before. Brigade "L" makes ready to support Brigade "A" in the battle as needed and to exploit the opening when the defenses of Rahfa fall apart. Brigade "E," held in readiness on the Beersheba road, engages in patrol actions against fedayeen groups coming over the border but is not yet alerted to advance on Gaza.

Eastern Axis. Brigade "D" starts its advance into enemy country via Kuntilla, which Brigade "X" has already captured.

4. 1 *November—D plus* 3.

Northern Axis. Having launched their attack in main around 0300 hours, Brigades "A" and "L" overrun the last defenses south of Rahfa by approximately 0900 hours. Brigade "A" holds within the works while Brigade "L" strikes westward along the coastal road, fighting through the afternoon and going into defensive position at sunset just a few miles east of El Arish. Late at night Brigade "E" is alerted to attack north at dawn against the defenses of Gaza, which are now cut off by the advance of Brigades "A" and "L."

Central Axis. Far overextended, Brigade "M" is now dealing with a highly fluid situation. The enemy-held two main ridges east of Abu Agueila are on its rear, while its two mobile combat teams maneuver westward along the Ismailia road in a half-successful attempt either to bring to battle or trap Egyptian armored forces east of the Canal. Repulsed but not badly hurt in an abortive attempt to take the Abu Agueila ridges by direct assault, Brigade "C" takes up a blocking position to the eastward.

Southern Axis. All operations are suspended and Brigade "X" rests.

Eastern Axis. Brigade "D" reaches its jump-off position on enemy soil just north of the Gulf of Aqaba.

5. 2 *November—D plus* 4.

Northern Axis. Brigade "L" captures El Arish in early morning and through the day continues its advance toward the Canal. Brigade "A" rests. Brigade "E" overruns the defenses outside Gaza through the morning, enters the city at noon, contrives an enemy surrender in mid-afternoon, and through the evening prepares for its final action, the capture of Khan Yunis, final point of resistance in the Gaza Strip.

Central Axis. Sometime during the night the Egyptian garrison abandons the two main ridges east of Abu Agueila and tries to get away to the north. Two combat teams of Brigade "M" continue pursuit of Egyptian armored forces westward toward the Canal. The other team refits.

Southern Axis. Brigade "X" advances westward toward Suez.

Eastern Axis. Brigade "D" gets within striking distance of Dahab.

6. *3 November—D plus 5.*

Southern Axis. Brigade "X," having crossed Sinai, now bends south along the coastal highway heading toward Sharm-El-Sheikh.

Eastern Axis. Brigade "D" continues its advance to the tip of Sinai.

Other Axes. Fighting operations are completed with the capture of Khan Yunis in the morning.

7. *4 November—D plus 6.*

Eastern Axis. Late in the day Brigade "D" penetrates the outer defenses of Sharm-El-Sheikh, then suspends the attack, awaiting the collection of its forces.

8. *5 November—D plus 7.*

Eastern Axis. Fighting operations in the Sinai war are completed with the capture of Sharm-El-Sheikh by Brigade "D" at 0900 hours.

Index

Index